The Kids Book of
CANADIAN IMMIGRATION

WRITTEN BY

Deborah Hodge

ILLUSTRATED BY

John Mantha

KIDS CAN PRESS

For the kids of Canada
and this diverse, wonderful land we live in

Acknowledgements

I wish to express my heartfelt gratitude and appreciation to the following people for their help in the creation of this book.

Dr. Harold M. Troper, Consultant, and Professor of the History of Education, University of Toronto, for his thorough review of my manuscript and for his clear guidance in issues relating to Canada's immigration past. His research and insights on Canadian social history and immigrant, ethnic and minority group history were invaluable.

The young people who so generously shared their stories of coming to Canada and described what it is like to be a new Canadian today. A special thanks to Alicia Henríquez and many students at Brentwood Park School, Edmonds Community School, Seaview Elementary School and Richmond Public Library.

The dedicated B.C. teachers and librarians who kindly put me in touch with their students: Kirsten Andersen, Sharon Freeman, Vicki Duncan, Kathy Richardson, Roger Beer and Sharon Domaas.

The adults who emigrated to Canada as children and allowed their personal stories and photographs to be used in the book: Robbie Waisman, Anna Kerz, Maurice Verkaar and Ted Taylor's daughter, Dulcie Doyle.

The talented people at Kids Can Press who believed in this project and put considerable time and energy into getting the book right, especially Valerie Wyatt and Sheila Barry, editors; Julia Naimska, designer; John Mantha, illustrator; Samantha Swenson, production editor; and Valerie Hussey, publisher.

Finally, I thank Dave and our family for making my writing life possible. — D.H.

The illustrator is indebted to the many painters and photographers who have documented Canada's immigrants. Extensive use has been made of these references to ensure accuracy and the right period feel. — J.M.

Kids Can Press acknowledges the financial support of the Government of Ontario, through the Ontario Media Development Corporation's Ontario Book Initiative; the Ontario Arts Council; the Canada Council for the Arts; and the Government of Canada, through the BPIDP, for our publishing activity.

Published in Canada by
Kids Can Press Ltd.
29 Birch Avenue
Toronto, ON M4V 1E2

Published in the U.S. by
Kids Can Press Ltd.
2250 Military Road
Tonawanda, NY 14150

www.kidscanpress.com

Edited by Valerie Wyatt and Sheila Barry
Designed by Julia Naimska
Printed and bound in China

The hardcover edition of this book is smyth sewn casebound.

CM 06 0 9 8 7 6 5 4 3 2 1

Library and Archives Canada Cataloguing in Publication

Hodge, Deborah
The kids book of Canadian immigration / written by Deborah Hodge ; illustrated by John Mantha.

ISBN-13: 978-1-55337-484-8
ISBN-10: 1-55337-484-3

1. Canada—Emigration and immigration—History—Juvenile literature. I. Mantha, John II. Title.

JV7220.H62 2006   j325.71   C2005-906796-9

Kids Can Press is a *Corus*™ Entertainment company

Credits
Every reasonable effort has been made to trace ownership of and give accurate credit to copyrighted material. Information that would enable the publisher to correct any discrepancies in future editions would be appreciated.

Photographs
p. 10: (*filles du roi*) Library and Archives Canada /C-020126; **p. 15:** (wood cutter) Library and Archives Canada /C-040162; **p. 27:** (head tax certificate) Library and Archives Canada /C-096443; **p. 33:** (poster) Library and Archives Canada /C-030621; **p. 41:** (signs) Canadian Jewish Congress National Archives, Montreal; **p. 43:** (war bride travel certificate) Pier 21 Society and the Nadeau family; **p. 47:** (passport) Courtesy Anna Kerz; **p. 57:** (poster) Reproduced with the permission of the Minister of Public Works and Government Services Canada, 2005.

Text
p. 18: (Archibald's Story) Excerpts from *On the Crofter's Trail: In Search of the Clearance Highlanders* by David Craig, published by Jonathan Cape, p. 27. Reprinted by permission of The Random House Group Ltd. **p. 19:** Excerpt from *Roughing It in the Bush or Life in Canada*, Volume I by Susanna Moodie, edited by Carl Ballstadt (Carlton University Press: 1990), pp. 83–85. **p. 21:** (Gerald's Diary) Excerpts from *The Untold Story: The Irish in Canada* by Robert O'Driscoll and Lorna Reynolds (Celtic Arts of Canada: 1988), pp. 111, 112. Reprinted with permission. **p. 23:** (Mrs. Little's Story) Excerpt from *The Narratives of Fugitive Slaves in Canada* by Benjamin Drew (Prospero Books: 2000, originally published 1856), p. 228. **p. 27:** (A Husband's Letter) Excerpt from *In a Strange Land: A Pictorial Record of the Chinese in Canada 1788–1923* by Richard Thomas Wright (Douglas & McIntyre: 1988), p. 34. **p. 29:** (One Man's Story) Excerpt from *Years of Sorry, Years of Shame* by Barry Broadfoot (Doubleday Canada: 1977), pp. 187–188. Reprinted with permission. **p. 31:** (Karm's Story and Mrs. Johl's Story) Excerpts from *Becoming Canadians: Pioneer Sikhs in Their Own Words* by Sarjeet Singh Jagpal (Harbour Publishing: 1997), pp. 39, 84. **p. 34:** (Sofie's Story) Excerpt from *Reminiscences of Courage and Hope: Stories of Ukrainian Canadian Women Pioneers* compiled by Peter Krawchuk, translation by Michael Ukas (Kobzar Publishing: 1991), p. 142. **p. 37:** (Robert's Story) Clapham, Robert. Written submission. Pier 21 National Historic Site. **p. 39:** (Kaarina's Story) Brooks, Kaarina. Written submission. Pier 21 National Historic Site. Reprinted with permission. **p. 39:** (Antonio's Story) Jiménez, Antonio Saez. Written submission. Pier 21 National Historic Site. Reprinted with permission. **p. 41:** (Turned Away!) Newspaper article excerpt from *Vancouver Sun*, 2 June 1939. Reprinted courtesy *Vancouver Sun*. **p. 43:** (Hilda's Story) Bradshaw, Hilda. Written submission. Pier 21 National Historic Site. Reprinted with permission. **p. 53:** (Rahim's Story) Excerpt from the Debates of the House of Commons of 2 October 2002. **p. 55:** (Vietnamese "Boat People") Newspaper article excerpt from "I Am One of the Boat People," *The Province* (Vancouver), 18 October 1983, p. 31. Reprinted courtesy of *The Province*.

CONTENTS

Welcome to Canada! 4

Canada's First People 6

Explorers and Furs 8

French Settlers 10

Loyalists 14

Early British Immigrants 16

Crossing the Atlantic 20

The Underground Railroad 22

West Coast Settlers 24

Early Asian Immigrants 26

Prairie Settlers 32

British Home Children 36

Pier 21 38

The War Years 40

Guest Children 42

War Brides 43

Jewish War Orphans 44

Displaced Persons and Refugees 46

Post-war Immigrants 48

Changing Times 50

Canada Opens Its Doors 54

Modern Times 56

Alicia's Story 58

Coming to Canada Today 60

Immigration Facts and Figures 62

Immigration Words 63

Index 64

WELCOME TO CANADA!

Step into a Canadian classroom today and you will find children of many different races, religions and nations. Some may be Aboriginal children whose ancestors have been in Canada for thousands of years. Some may be French Canadians, descended from people who sailed from France more than 400 years ago.

Many will be children born in Canada, but whose parents, grandparents or great-grandparents came from Britain, Europe or other countries of the world. And some children will be brand new Canadians from China, India, Pakistan, Korea, the Philippines, the Middle East, the Caribbean and many other places.

Our country is like a big version of this classroom. It is home to over 32 million people from a wide range of backgrounds and origins. It has two official languages, English and French, but many more are spoken. People of more than 200 cultures live and work here in harmony.

Canada is a multicultural country — a country of many cultures. How did this happen? Most Canadians are immigrants or the descendants of immigrants — people who came here from other countries. Some settled in Canada a long time ago, while others arrived yesterday. No matter when they came or where they came from, people of many nations now call Canada home.

Why do people come to Canada? In the world, Canada is seen as a fair country where people are considered equal regardless of their religion, skin colour or language. Canada does not have the history of war, violence and devastating poverty sometimes found in other countries. It provides a safe haven for those fleeing difficult and dangerous situations. And it allows people to make a new start in a new land — there are schools, jobs and opportunities to earn a living.

But Canada hasn't always welcomed newcomers. At times in Canada's past, only people of certain races or countries were allowed to come here, while others were banned. Today, Canada accepts people from around the world, including refugees in need of safety. Through immigration, Canada has become a wonderfully diverse land. This is the story of Canada's people: who they are and how they came to be here.

These students are in Grade 4 and 5 in Vancouver. Some of them were born in Canada. Many others come from countries around the world.

Who is included?

People from so many cultures (more than 200) live in Canada that we simply didn't have the space to include them all in this book. We recognize the contributions of people from every race, faith and origin to our diverse and vibrant nation.

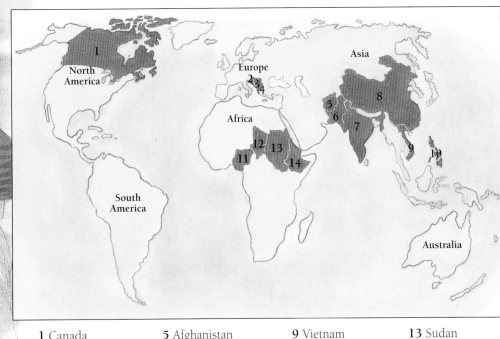

1 Canada	5 Afghanistan	9 Vietnam	13 Sudan
2 Croatia	6 Pakistan	10 Philippines	14 Ethiopia
3 Bosnia	7 India	11 Nigeria	
4 Serbia	8 China	12 Chad	

The kids on these two pages come from the countries labelled on this map.

CANADA'S FIRST PEOPLE

Scientists suggest that Aboriginal people were Canada's first arrivals — that they travelled from Asia by crossing a wide bridge of land that once joined Siberia and Alaska. Aboriginal people, on the other hand, believe that they have always lived here — since time immemorial, a time before anyone can remember.

Either way, for thousands of years, the Aboriginal people were the only inhabitants of Canada. They lived in different regions of the country and adapted their lives to suit the climate and resources of each area.

People in the Far North hunted sea mammals and built snowhomes. People of the Northwest Coast fished for salmon and travelled in canoes carved from huge cedar trees. And Plains people criss-crossed the prairies with portable homes, following the buffalo they hunted for food.

By A.D. 1000, there were about 350 000 Aboriginal people in Canada. Then small groups of Europeans began to arrive. The way of life for Aboriginal people began to change as newcomers explored the country and settled in it.

The Aboriginal people faced many difficult challenges from the newcomers. Over time, Aboriginal people were forced to give up their customs and traditional ways of life. The government and settlers also took away lands that had long been the home of Aboriginal people and moved many of them onto reserves. Starting in the 1880s, many Aboriginal children were taken from their families to live in residential schools. Here, the children were made to speak English and adopt British or European ways.

These were devastating events for the Aboriginal people, and they are still working hard to recover from them. Today, they have strong organizations to help them reclaim their lands and customs, and get compensation for the injustices of the past.

Canadians of Aboriginal heritage today:
more than one million, living in every province and territory of the country

Northwest Coast Aboriginal people travelled the ocean in canoes carved from cedar trees.

Dr. Freda Ahenakew was a professor of Native Studies and a leader in the vital work of preserving Aboriginal languages. She received the Order of Canada for recording the stories of her people and ensuring the survival of the Plains Cree language and culture.

Leonard Marchand was one of the first Aboriginal Members of Parliament and the first federal Aboriginal Cabinet Minister. He was also appointed to the Senate in 1984. He received the Order of Canada for representing and seeking justice for Aboriginal people.

Louis Riel was a strong and determined leader of the Métis — people of Aboriginal and European descent. In Manitoba in the mid-1800s, Riel led the fight for Métis land rights and against injustices of the government.

The Vikings: First Europeans in Canada

About 1000 years ago, the first Europeans came to Canada. They were called the Norse or Vikings and they sailed from Scandinavia in long ships searching for new farmlands and other riches. A Viking named Leif Ericsson is believed to be the first European to set foot on the mainland in North America.

In about 1004, a group of 160 Vikings settled briefly at L'Anse aux Meadows on Newfoundland's Great Northern Peninsula. They brought cattle and built sod-walled homes. A Norse woman named Gudrid gave birth to a son, Snorri, the first non-Aboriginal child born in Canada.

But, the Vikings didn't stay. The winters were harsh and food was scarce. They fought with one another and with the Aboriginal people. After several difficult years, the Vikings returned to Europe. Today, all that is left of them are the remains of their settlement.

These are the remains of the Viking settlement at L'Anse aux Meadows.

EXPLORERS AND FURS

After the Vikings, it was another 500 years before other Europeans came to Canada. These people were the explorers who sailed west across the Atlantic Ocean hoping to find a quick route to Asia, with its valuable silks and spices. But the explorers didn't get to Asia. They reached Canada instead, paving the way for European settlers to follow in later years.

John Cabot

John Cabot set sail from England in 1497 and likely landed on the coast of Newfoundland, Labrador or Cape Breton. He claimed the area for England. His news of rich fishing

grounds spread, prompting fishermen from other European countries to follow him. English, French, Portuguese, Spanish and Basque ships all began fishing off the coast of Newfoundland in the 1500s.

Jacques Cartier

Jacques Cartier crossed the Atlantic in 1534, sent by the King of France to find gold or a sea route to Asia. Instead, he found himself in the Gulf of St. Lawrence. Cartier planted a wooden cross on the Gaspé Peninsula and claimed the region for France. The Iroquois and their chief, Donnacona, who had come to the area to fish, were angered by this act. Later, they relented and were helpful to Cartier and his crew.

Cartier made two other journeys to Canada and further explored the St. Lawrence River. Through his travels, and in discussions with the Iroquois, Cartier began to understand that the mighty river led inland into a huge country. His discovery encouraged other explorers to venture more deeply into Canada.

Samuel de Champlain

Samuel de Champlain came to Canada from France in 1603. He was an explorer and cartographer (mapmaker). He published the first modern-looking map of eastern Canada. He also helped set up the first trading posts and French settlements in Canada. In 1608, he built a *habitation* (settlement) at what is now Quebec City. This was the beginning of New France — a colony of French people who settled permanently in Canada.

Champlain dreamed of making the colony large and strong. He formed trading partnerships with the Huron and other Aboriginal people and developed the fur trade. Champlain is often called "The Father of New France."

Fur Trade

The explorers didn't find gold, but they did discover something almost as valuable — furs. Beavers were plentiful in Canada, and European traders came here to exchange goods with the Aboriginal people for beaver furs. The traders shipped the furs to Europe, where they were made into silky, soft hats that were the height of fashion.

France and England were deeply involved in the fur trade. For many years, they battled for control of the industry. Both England and France set up forts and colonies (settlements) in Canada to be close to the furs. The fur trade went on for nearly 200 years and was a powerful factor in attracting European attention to Canada.

Furs were exchanged at trading posts throughout Canada. Many of these posts later developed into Canada's earliest towns.

The under-fur next to the beaver's skin was processed to become felt, then the felt was shaped into hats. Here are some styles of hats that were popular in Europe in the 1800s.

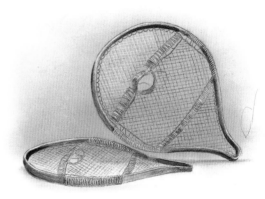

Aboriginal people showed European traders how to travel using toboggans, birchbark canoes and these beaver tail snowshoes. The people also acted as wilderness guides and interpreters.

FRENCH SETTLERS

The French were the first Europeans to settle permanently in Canada. The area they settled was called New France, a colony ruled by the King of France.

In the early years, there were only a handful of *habitants* (French settlers) in New France — fewer than 3000 in 1663. The population grew very slowly. So the King of France, who wanted a large and prosperous colony, sent soldiers there. In addition to the soldiers came clerks and men who worked at such jobs as carpentry, masonry, land clearing, house building and so on.

The Hébert Family's Story

Marie Rollet, Louis Hébert and their three children were a French family who settled in Quebec City in 1617. They were the first known family to cultivate land in Canada. Louis Hébert was both an apothecary (an expert in the use of healing plants) and a colonist. Marie and Louis' daughter, Anne, is believed to have been the first European woman to marry in Canada. A monument in Quebec City commemorates this first family of New France.

This is an artist's vision of **les filles du roi**. In real life, they did not wear such grand clothing.

Les Filles du Roi

As well as men, New France needed women, too. So the King sent about 800 young unmarried women from France to become the wives of soldiers. Some were as young as 14. Many were poor and had little or no family. Upon their marriage, some received a dowry — a small amount of money or a gift of household items — from the King.

Called *les filles du roi* — daughters of the King — these women often came to have large families of 10 or more children. By 1695, the French colony had grown to almost 13 000 people. By 1763, there were about 70 000 people in New France, most of whom had been born there.

Jeanne's Story

Jeanne Fauconnier was only 17 years old when she sailed from France to Canada in the late 1600s. She was the daughter of a cobbler (shoemaker) who had died, leaving her alone in the world.

The trip across the Atlantic Ocean took several weeks. As her ship neared Canada, the land must have looked wild and cold — a far cry from the bustling France she had left behind. Yet it was the beginning of Jeanne's new life. In just a few weeks, she would be married.

Jeanne Fauconnier was one of hundreds of *les filles du roi* who came to Canada between 1663 and 1673.

How the *Habitants* Lived

The *habitants* spoke French, practised the Catholic religion and followed French customs. Most *habitants* lived under the seigneurial system — a system of land distribution modelled on a similar one in France. The King of France gave large blocks of land called seigneuries to seigneurs (landlords), and they, in turn, leased some of their land to *habitants*. Under this system, a *habitant* had to build a house, farm his strip of land and pay rent to the seigneur.

Habitants had to produce almost everything they needed. They made clothes from the wool and flax they grew. They cultivated their own food and hunted and fished. They also

built homes, barns and furniture with wood they cut from the forest.

A family often lived in a one-room wooden building that had no indoor toilet or running water.

A large stone fireplace was used for cooking and heating the house. Usually, the children helped their parents with the work and didn't go to school.

Townspeople

While most French settlers lived on farms, some also lived in the towns of New France — Quebec (now Quebec City), Montreal and Trois-Rivières. Much of the business of New France took place in the towns.

Montreal was becoming a great centre for the fur trade. Quebec was the administrative capital of New France and the main port for trade with France. Quebec was also where immigrants arrived and travellers departed.

Fur-trading merchants, artisans and craftspeople lived in the towns. So did wealthy and important people, such as the bishop and governor. Hospitals, schools and religious institutions, also in the towns, were run by Catholic nuns and priests.

Acadians

There were also French settlers in Acadia (now Nova Scotia). Started in 1604, Acadia was the first permanent French colony in North America. (However, throughout its history, the colony was claimed in turn by France and England.)

The Acadians traded with other settlements for goods they did not make themselves.

In the early years, there were few Acadians — about 400 by 1671. These early settlers were very resourceful. They farmed, kept livestock and hunted, fished and trapped. The population of Acadia grew steadily over time. By 1711, there were some 2500 people and by 1755, more than 13 000 Acadians.

Canadians of French heritage today:
nearly five million, with most living in Quebec. Most French Canadians speak French — one of Canada's official languages (English is the other).

Canadians of Acadian heritage today:
about 70 000

War!

During the 1700s, France and England were often at war with each other. Their battles spread to North America.

From 1755 to 1762, the Acadians were pushed off their land by British soldiers. (Acadians refused to take an oath of loyalty to Britain.) Acadian homes were burned and the people were forced onto ships that sailed for France, England and the United States. Of the 13 000 Acadians who lived in the region,

some 10 000 were deported, while the rest fled. Some hid in the woods for years. Those who stayed in the area (or left and later returned) kept the Acadian culture alive.

In New France, the British won a key battle called The Battle of the Plains of Abraham (fought at Quebec in 1759). As a result, the French turned over control of New France to the British and by 1763, the vast French colonies were under British rule. At first, the British tried to force the French settlers to adapt to English culture. But the settlers resisted, and French culture and language has remained strong in Canada ever since.

The British forced thousands of Acadians to leave their homes and sail to other countries.

CANADIAN OF ACADIAN HERITAGE

Antonine Maillet is an award-winning author of novels, plays, radio and television scripts and children's books about Acadian people and their history. Through her storytelling, she has helped keep the culture of Acadian people alive.

CANADIANS OF FRENCH HERITAGE

Jeanne Sauvé was the first female federal Cabinet Minister from Quebec, the first woman Speaker of the House of Commons and the first female Governor General. She was a keen supporter of issues involving women's rights, youth and world peace.

Pierre Elliott Trudeau was the Prime Minister of Canada from 1968 to 1979 and from 1980 to 1984. He introduced Canada's Multiculturalism Policy and the Official Languages Act, which made French and English the two official languages of Canada.

LOYALISTS

From 1775 to 1783, a war called the American Revolution raged in eastern North America. Fighting on one side were the Patriots, people who no longer wanted to be ruled by Britain. On the other side were the Loyalists, who were loyal to Britain. The Loyalists were a diverse group that included people of British, Black, Aboriginal and German origins.

In the end, the Patriots won and formed a new country, which they called the United States of America. The Loyalists were seen as traitors and many were driven out. Their homes and farms were confiscated or burned. Some Loyalists were punished by being covered in hot tar and feathers. Others were jailed or even hanged.

About 40 000 Loyalists fled to Canada. Some settled in areas in present-day Quebec and Ontario. Others went to the Maritime regions — now Nova Scotia, New Brunswick and Prince Edward Island.

When the Loyalists arrived in Canada, they had lost everything. Britain rewarded them by giving them land and food and supplies for three years. They cleared the land, built homes and farmed.

Over time, the Loyalists carved out a new life and helped to create schools, churches, government institutions and settlements that attracted other British people to Canada.

Fearing for their lives and safety, thousands of Loyalists came to Canada.

This is a painting of a wood cutter from Shelburne, Nova Scotia, in 1788.

Rose's Story

Rose Fortune was about 10 years old when she came to Nova Scotia in 1784. She earned money by meeting ships at the Annapolis wharf and hauling passengers' bags in her wheelbarrow. As Rose got older, she began a trucking and moving company that her descendants still run today. Rose was also the first policewoman in Canada.

Black Loyalists

About 3500 Black Loyalists sailed to Nova Scotia from New York at the end of the American Revolution. The Black Loyalists had been slaves in the colonies and Britain promised them freedom if they would fight on the Loyalist side. Many settled in a Black community called Birchtown, near Shelburne, Nova Scotia. Some also settled in New Brunswick, while others went to Upper or Lower Canada (now Ontario and Quebec).

The Black Loyalists expected the same rewards given to all Loyalists — land, food and supplies. But Britain didn't follow through on all of its promises. Black Loyalists received smaller parcels of land than White Loyalists (about half the size), and many didn't receive any land at all. Unable to make a living from farming, these Black Loyalists were forced to work for White employers who often mistreated them. Many suffered from poverty and discrimination. In 1792, about a third of the Black Loyalists left for Sierra Leone, Africa, to seek a better life.

Today, the Black Loyalists Heritage Society and museum, located in Birchtown, is dedicated to preserving the history of the Black Loyalists. (In 1784, Birchtown had the largest population of free Black people outside of Africa.) Some descendants of the Black Loyalists still live in the area.

BLACK LOYALIST

Colonel Stephen Blucke led an all-Black regiment fighting on the side of the British during the American Revolution. After the war, he settled in Birchtown and became an important leader in the Black Loyalist community. He was a magistrate, teacher and leader of public construction in the area.

CANADIAN OF BLACK LOYALIST HERITAGE

Daurene Lewis was the first Black woman mayor in Nova Scotia and in North America. She received the Order of Canada in 2002 for her work in race relations, the advancement of women in business and the promotion of the arts. She is a descendant of Rose Fortune.

EARLY BRITISH IMMIGRANTS

Although the British were among the first Europeans to come to Canada, their numbers were small until Britain took over New France in 1763. But by the 1800s, large numbers of immigrants from Ireland, Scotland, England and Wales began to arrive. Many were trying to escape difficult conditions in their own countries.

These Irish people are in Liverpool waiting to board the ship that will take them to Canada.

Irish Immigrants

The largest group were the Irish immigrants. Most came to get away from terrible hunger and poverty in Ireland during the Great Potato Famine of the late 1840s. The potato crop, which most people depended on for food, had been destroyed by disease. Many thousands of people died of starvation. Sometimes, entire villages were wiped out. Up to two million people fled Ireland. Hundreds of thousands boarded crowded ships for North America.

By the 1850s, over 500 000 Irish immigrants had come to Canada.

Most settled in cities and towns. By 1871, they were the biggest ethnic group in every large city and town except Montreal and Quebec City.

Many Irish immigrants worked as labourers, often in construction and public works, and helped Canada expand and grow. In spite of their contribution to Canada, they suffered because of low wages, poverty and discrimination. The rest of the population shunned the Irish for the poor and crowded conditions in which they had to live. Thousands of Irish immigrants later left for the United States.

> **Canadians of Irish heritage today:**
> nearly four million, living in every province and territory of the country

Scottish Immigrants

Between 1770 and 1815, about 15 000 Scottish Highlanders came to Canada from Scotland. Many were farmers who had been forced off their lands by landlords who wanted to raise sheep and produce wool for the new factories. This was a dark time in Scottish history called the "Clearances."

Without land or homes, the Highlanders chose to immigrate to Canada. They settled mainly in Prince Edward Island, Nova Scotia and Upper Canada (now Ontario). Some also went to the Red River colony in what is now Manitoba. Wherever they lived, they held on to their Scottish language (Gaelic) and customs.

Between 1815 and 1870, another 170 000 Scottish settlers of diverse backgrounds came to Canada. In addition to Highlanders, many of these later settlers were from the Lowlands area of Scotland. Most were farmers and craftspeople, while others were professional and business people. These newcomers spoke English instead of Gaelic.

Large numbers of Scottish immigrants continued to arrive after 1870 and throughout the 1900s. The Scottish were very active in politics and business — especially in the fur and lumber trades, banking and railway management. They also started many schools.

Archibald's Story

As a young man, Archibald Geikie witnessed a group of travellers who had been forced off their land during the Clearances. He remembered, "I could see a long and motley procession winding along the road … There were old men and women, too feeble to walk, who were placed in carts; the younger members of the community on foot were carrying their bundles of clothes and household effects, while the children with looks of alarm, walked alongside. When they set forth … a cry of grief went up to heaven … the sound seemed to re-echo through the whole wide valley … in one prolonged note of desolation."

Canadians of Scottish heritage today:
over four million people of Scottish descent

English Immigrants

Thousands of English immigrants came to Canada in the 1800s. The cities in England were overcrowded and many people were poor, so the British government encouraged them to leave for Canada. Ordinary people and officials, such as governors, judges and army officers, came to Canada. By 1906, over 110 000 immigrants from England had settled here.

The English settlers had a powerful and lasting influence in Canada. Our laws, politics and many of our customs and practices are based on the British system. English is also one of our official languages.

Susanna's Story

Among the English settlers was the wealthy Moodie family: Susanna and Dunbar Moodie and their baby, Catherine. The Moodies came to Canada in 1832. Like many other newcomers, they were completely unprepared for the rough conditions of living in the Canadian wilderness.

On first seeing her home in the backwoods of Upper Canada, near today's Cobourg, Ontario, Susanna Moodie wrote: "I gazed upon the place in perfect dismay, for I had never seen a shed called a house before. 'You must be mistaken [said Susanna to her driver]; this is not a house, but a cattle-shed or a pig-sty'... I could only stare at the place, with my eyes swimming in tears ... A room with but one ... window ... not an article of furniture to be seen ... The rain poured in at the open door, beat in at the shattered window, and dropped upon our heads from the holes in the roof. The wind blew keenly from a thousand apertures [gaps] in the log walls; and nothing could exceed the uncomfortableness of our situation."

But the Moodies were lucky — their home was already built. Most people had to clear the land and then build their homes.

Canadians of English heritage today:
about six million

Nellie McClung was a women's rights activist who fought to get western Canadian women the right to vote. She was also a lecturer, author, the first female member of the CBC Board of Governors and a delegate to the League of Nations (a forerunner to the United Nations).

Sir John A. Macdonald was one of the Fathers of Confederation and Canada's first Prime Minister from 1867 to 1873 and later from 1878 to 1891. He helped unite Canada by building the first transcontinental railway (the Canadian Pacific Railway) across the country.

Irene Parlby battled to have women declared "persons" under the law, allowing them to hold political office. She was the first female Cabinet Minister in Alberta and the second female Cabinet Minister in the British Commonwealth.

Gregory Scofield is a poet, storyteller, activist and community worker who has won important awards for his writing. Like many other Canadians today, he has mixed heritage. His ancestors are Scottish, English, Cree and French.

CROSSING THE ATLANTIC

Immigrants coming to Canada from Europe in the early 1800s travelled by sailing ship. The journey across the Atlantic Ocean was often difficult and dangerous.

Immigrants with little money sailed on overcrowded ships in horrific conditions. The trip could take 6 to 12 weeks. Rough seas made many people seasick. Ships were sometimes wrecked in violent storms and people drowned.

More often, diseases, such as cholera, typhus and dysentery, took the lives of many passengers. The diseases were spread through bad sanitation or contaminated water and food. In 1847 alone, some 9000 immigrants (mostly poor Irish) died during the Atlantic crossing. Most were buried at sea. Another 10 000 people died upon reaching Canada. Many Irish children whose parents had died were adopted by French families in Quebec.

Passengers were crowded together for weeks in ships that sailed across the Atlantic.

Grosse Île

Authorities did not want the diseases to spread to Canada. New immigrants were taken from their ships at Grosse Île, an island in the St. Lawrence River, not far from Quebec City. There, they were examined before they were allowed to enter Canada. Those who were sick stayed on the island until they recovered — or died.

More than 5000 Irish immigrants were buried on the island. A monument erected in their honour says: "Sacred to the memory of thousands of Irish immigrants who to preserve the faith, suffered hunger and exile in 1847–48, and stricken with fever, ended here their sorrowful pilgrimmage …"

These people died on the ship and are being buried at sea.

Gerald's Diary

In 1895, the diary of Gerald Keegan was published. According to the diary, he was an Irish schoolteacher who came to Canada on an immigrant ship in 1847 and died soon after. People have recently begun to doubt that the diary is real. Instead, it may be a novel based on what was happening at the time. Even so, people agree that his picture of life on board ship is very true to life.

Gerald Keegan described the ship, which had room for 200 to 300 passengers. Instead, 600 people had been packed on board, huddled together in the ship's hold (bottom), where cargo was usually stowed. They lived on rotting food and dirty water. The air was stale and smelled bad, especially when people got sick. There were no toilets, only buckets that were emptied into the sea.

The diary entry on April 17, 1847, said, "Biscuits for three days were served. They were … very mouldy … Bad as they were, they were eagerly accepted, and so hungry were the people that by night most of them were eaten. How shamefully the ship was overcrowded … There were not berths for two-thirds of the passengers, and … they were given up to the women and the children. The others slept on chests and bundles and many could find no other resting place than the floor, which was so occupied that there was no room left to walk."

The April 21, 1847, entry said, "The first death took place last night, when a boy of five years succumbed to dysentery. In the afternoon, a wail suddenly arose from the hold — a fine young woman had died from the same cause. Both were dropped into the sea at sunset."

These Irish orphans are meeting the French family who will care for them.

THE UNDERGROUND RAILROAD

After the Black Loyalists arrived, Black people didn't come to Canada in large numbers again until the Underground Railroad brought fleeing slaves from the United States.

The Underground Railroad was a secret network of trails and safe houses that took escaping slaves from the southern states to Canada from about 1840 to 1860. It was operated by both Black and White people who were angry about the treatment of slaves. "Conductors" guided the slaves to safe "stations." "Station agents" hid the slaves in their homes and barns, gave them food and pointed the way north to Canada and freedom. The code word for fugitives was "cargo" or "freight." Using a code helped keep the slaves, and those who hid them, safe.

Fugitive slaves travelled at night and hid by day to avoid slave hunters who would return them to their owners for a fee. Returned slaves were severely punished. The trip to Canada could take weeks or even months. The slaves had little food or money and risked everything to escape to Canada.

Once here, the slaves were free. They built homes and schools and established new lives. Sadly, many still faced discrimination and hardship. A great number returned to the United States in 1865 at the end of the Civil War, when all American slaves were declared free. No one knows how many slaves came to Canada on the railroad, but it could be as many as 100 000.

Canadians of Black heritage today:
more than 600 000, with most living in Montreal and Toronto. Some are Canadian-born. Others are recently from Africa, Central and South America, the Caribbean and the United States.

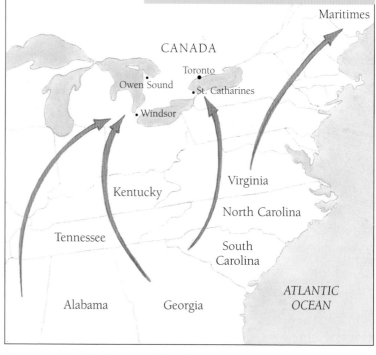

Routes of the Underground Railway

Mrs. Little's Story

Mr. and Mrs. John Little were slaves who escaped to Canada from the United States in the 1840s. They had to walk, and at times even swim, with their belongings on their backs. Remembering their escape, Mrs. Little said, "My shoes gave out before many days, — then I wore my husband's old shoes till they were used up. Then we came on barefooted … My feet were blistered and sore and my ankles swollen; but I had to keep on … I was scared all but to death … We never slept at the same time; while one slept, the other kept watch … If we had [slept at the same time], we would not have reached Canada."

CANADIANS OF BLACK HERITAGE

Harriet's Story

Harriet Tubman was a famous Black conductor on the Underground Railroad. She led more slaves to freedom than anyone else. Harriet was born into slavery in 1820 in the United States. At age seven, she tried to escape but was caught and severely beaten. When she was about 30 years old, she successfully escaped. Later, she guided at least 300 other slaves to freedom in Canada. Harriet dressed as a man to disguise herself. She was never caught and she never lost anyone in her care.

Mary Ann Shadd came to Canada from the United States in 1851 and started a school for escaped slaves. During her life, she was a teacher, lawyer, Black-rights activist and the first Black woman to publish a newspaper in North America.

Lincoln Alexander was the first Black federal Cabinet Minister in Canada and the first Black Lieutenant Governor of Ontario. He received the Order of Canada for his work on behalf of young people and in social justice and race relations.

WEST COAST SETTLERS

Europeans did not come to the west coast of Canada until the late 1700s — more than 150 years after the first French settlers arrived in eastern Canada.

First to come were the explorers. Juan Pérez Hernández, Captain James Cook and Captain George Vancouver travelled up the coast, while Alexander MacKenzie, David Thompson and Simon Fraser explored the interior of British Columbia.

Simon Fraser and his men built important trading centres, such as Fort McLeod (in 1805), Fort St. James (1806) and Fort George (1807), that paved the way for Britain's claim to the West. A busy fur trade developed and, in 1849, the British colony of Vancouver Island was established.

Other than a handful of French, American and British settlers who lived around Fort Victoria, Fort Vancouver and other trading posts, few immigrants had yet come to British Columbia. That would change with the discovery of gold.

Gold Rush!
In 1858, as many as 30 000 people, mostly Americans, rushed to British Columbia's Fraser River. Word had leaked out that gold had been discovered. A second gold rush in the Cariboo from 1860 to 1866 drew more people hoping to get rich. Most didn't find gold and left soon after. But those who stayed began farming, logging and started businesses.

The gold rushes changed the population of British Columbia. In addition to the 25 000 Aboriginal people already in B.C., there were now 1500 Chinese people (read more about them on pages 26–27), 500 Black people and 8000 White people living in the region.

More settlers arrived after the Canadian Pacific Railway was completed in 1885. And British Columbia's natural resources (logging, mining, fishing and farming) also attracted people, mainly from Britain or other places in Canada. By 1900, more than half of British Columbia's population was of British descent.

Black Settlers

Black Californians were invited to come to Vancouver Island (Britain's first colony on the west coast) by Governor James Douglas. Douglas wanted hard-working, educated settlers who would set up mines, mills and fishing operations. In 1858, 400 Black families sailed to Victoria from San Francisco. Most opened businesses in Victoria, but a few also went to the gold rush. At the end of the American Civil War, many of these settlers returned to the United States.

Hawaiian Settlers

In the 1800s, about 500 people came from Hawaii to work in the fur trade, mainly at coastal trading posts. They called themselves "Kanakas" — Hawaiian for "human beings" — and formed their own small settlements. Some men married Aboriginal women and stayed in British Columbia. They cleared land, built cabins, fished and grew their own food. Descendants of some of these early settlers still live on British Columbia's Gulf Islands today.

The Schubert Family's Story

It was 1862 and, like thousands of other goldseekers, Catherine and Augustus Schubert hoped to strike it rich. They travelled with their children, Gus, aged five, Mary Jane, three, and James, one, mostly on foot from Fort Garry, near today's Winnipeg, to the goldfields of British Columbia. Catherine, who was born in Ireland, and Augustus, a German immigrant, had met in the United States before coming to Canada.

The family went with a group of 150 men called the Overlanders. Catherine was the only woman. During the five-month journey, the family endured rough conditions,

Catherine Schubert and her family trekked across Canada to the goldfields of British Columbia.

fierce weather and near starvation. They cut trails through forests, hiked over mountain passes and rafted down rivers. Hours after arriving in Kamloops, British Columbia, Catherine gave birth to a baby girl named Rose.

The family didn't find gold, but they stayed in British Columbia and began farming. Today, a monument honours Catherine Schubert as one of the province's earliest settlers.

Black Californians were some of the early settlers in Victoria.

EARLY ASIAN IMMIGRANTS

From the mid-1800s to the early 1900s, people from China, Japan and India came across the Pacific Ocean by ship to British Columbia.

For these early immigrants, Canada was not a welcoming place. They were paid less than other workers, kept from working in many professions and not allowed to vote.

Chinese Immigrants

About 7000 Chinese people came to British Columbia during the gold rushes, but the population shrank to about 1500 when the gold rushes ended. Those who stayed (almost all men) found jobs. They cleared land, mined coal or worked in restaurants, laundries, salmon-canning factories and as servants in family homes.

More Chinese men came to help build the British Columbia section of Canadian Pacific Railway (CPR) from 1880 to 1885. They wanted to earn money to support their families in China, and the CPR wanted labourers who would work hard for little pay.

The Chinese workers were reliable and hard-working men, yet they faced terrible discrimination. They had to live in camps apart from other workers and were often given the most difficult and dangerous jobs. At least 600 Chinese men died working on the railway. Those who survived were paid less than the other workers, and when the railway was finished, most could not afford to return to China. Many stayed in British Columbia and opened laundries, tailor shops, restaurants and other businesses.

The government made it difficult for more Chinese people to come to Canada. In 1885, a "head tax" (entry to Canada tax) of $50 was required from all new Chinese immigrants.

In 1900, the tax was raised to $100 and in 1903 to $500. (At that time, most Chinese workers earned less than a dollar a day.) The tax made it virtually impossible for the workers to bring their wives and children to Canada. In 1923, the tax was removed but replaced with the Chinese Immigration Act, which restricted almost all Chinese immigration.

Chinese immigrants lost the right to vote in 1875 and could not vote again until 1947. They also suffered from discrimination and acts of mob violence. (Read about the anti-Asian riot on page 28.)

The Chinese Immigration Act was withdrawn in 1947, but it wasn't until 1967 that the last restrictions against Chinese immigration were lifted.

This head tax certificate proved that the bearer had paid the tax to enter Canada.

These people lived in Vancouver's early Chinatown.

A Husband's Letter

A Husband's Letter

After the head tax was imposed, Chinese men could not afford to bring their wives and families to Canada. Many men never saw their families again. Here is part of a letter written by a man to his wife in China:

My beloved wife;
It has been several autumns since [I] left you for a far remote alien land … Yesterday I received another of your letters. I could not keep the tears from running down my cheeks … Because of our destitution [poverty in China] I went out to try to make a living … I am detained in this secluded corner of a strange land … I wish this paper would console you a little. This is all I can do for now.

Canadians of Chinese heritage today:
over one million, living in every province and territory, with the largest numbers in British Columbia and Ontario

CANADIANS OF CHINESE HERITAGE

Adrienne Clarkson, a former broadcaster and journalist, was the first person of Chinese descent to be Governor General of Canada. She received the Order of Canada and has been a strong supporter of the arts, journalism and many charities.

Paul Yee is an award-winning author of historical fiction for young readers. Many of his books are based on the experiences of early Chinese Canadians and were inspired by his work as a volunteer in Vancouver's Chinatown.

Japanese Immigrants

Japanese immigrants (almost all men) first came to Canada from 1877 to 1907. They left poor, overcrowded villages in Japan to find work here and send money home to their families. Many had planned to return to Japan, and when they couldn't, they sent for wives and families to join them in Canada.

By 1914, there were 10 000 Japanese people here. Many settled in or around Vancouver and Victoria or other places on the Pacific coast. Most worked in fishing, mining, forestry or railway construction. Some also farmed.

Like the Chinese immigrants, the Japanese faced discrimination. They too were not allowed to vote or hold certain jobs, and they were paid less than other workers.

The Canadian government slowed then halted Japanese immigration from 1907 to 1967. When the last restriction on their immigration was lifted in 1967, a second wave of Japanese immigrants began to arrive in Canada.

Riot!

On September 7, 1907, an angry mob stormed into the Japanese and Chinese parts of Vancouver, breaking windows and threatening people. Stores and businesses were damaged by thousands of protesters who wanted to stop employers from bringing in immigrants from Asia who would work for cheaper wages. The riot ended when the Japanese Canadians fought back. (An earlier riot against the Chinese had taken place in 1887.)

Windows were broken and shops were damaged in the riot of 1907.

Relocation

World War II broke out in 1939. When Japanese planes attacked Pearl Harbor, Hawaii, in 1941, the United States entered the war. Fears arose that people of Japanese descent living in the United States and on Canada's west coast would help the enemy. So in 1942, nearly 22 000 Japanese Canadians were uprooted from their homes and relocated (forced to move to other places).

Most people were sent to relocation camps in the interior of British Columbia. Some also went to farms in Alberta, Manitoba and Ontario. Still others worked on road crews in British Columbia or went to prisoner-of-war camps in Ontario. They lost their homes, farms and

Many Japanese immigrants worked in the fishing industry and owned their own boats. This is an early salmon fishing boat.

fishing boats. Families were split up, and many lost their life-savings.

The relocation camps (often set in mining ghost towns) were crowded and uncomfortable. Some people had to spend the first winter in tents before constructing small shacks, to be shared by several families. Others lived in abandoned buildings. Many times there was no running water, heat or electricity. People often had to grow their own food.

In 1945, Japanese Canadians were forced to choose between leaving Canada for Japan or moving east of the Rocky Mountains. Most went to the prairies, Ontario or Quebec.

In 1949, Japanese Canadians were allowed to return to the west coast and permitted to vote. In 1988, the government formally apologized to Japanese Canadians and paid them compensation for their relocation and other injustices during World War II.

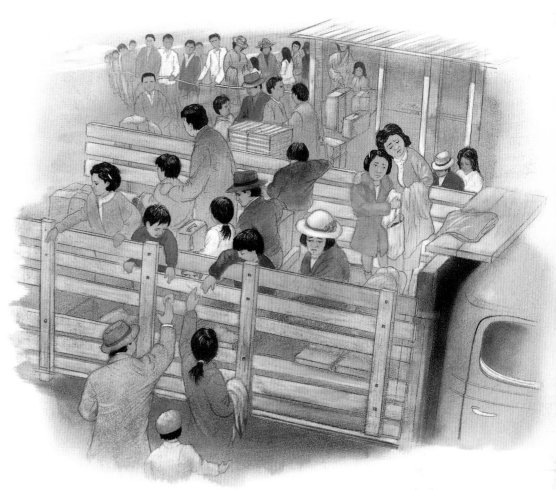

Most people taken from their homes had been born in Canada, including many children. No one was ever found to have had ties with the "enemy."

CANADIANS OF JAPANESE HERITAGE

Joy Kogawa is an award-winning poet and author of books for children and adults. She wrote *Naomi's Road*, a story about a girl in a relocation camp. Joy was seven when she and her family were relocated to a camp in Slocan, British Columbia.

David Suzuki is a scientist, writer, environmentalist and television host. He has spent years educating people about environmental issues. David was six when he and his family were sent to Slocan. Joy Kogawa was his classmate there.

One Man's Story

A Vancouver dentist, who was relocated with his wife and daughter to the Greenwood camp, remembered: "Greenwood … was a ghost town then. Each family had one room … some families had five and six children … This was in an old hotel and there was one toilet on each floor … the stove was in the centre of the hall … and with all the families … it was terribly crowded. And, my it was cold. One day it went to 39 below and the stove couldn't hope to heat [us] … people woke up with frost … on their blankets … shoes were frozen to the floor."

Canadians of Japanese heritage today:
about 75 000, living mainly in British Columbia and Ontario

Passengers on the Komagata Maru were sent back to India.

South Asian Immigrants

The first South Asian immigrants were men from India, Pakistan, Sri Lanka and Bangladesh who came to British Columbia from 1904 to 1908 looking for jobs. Many worked in sawmills, while others farmed or did railway construction.

By 1908, there were more than 5000 South Asians here. Like the early Chinese and Japanese immigrants, South Asians were made to feel unwelcome and faced discrimination under the law. They too could not vote and were barred from many jobs.

The Canadian government also tried to stop more South Asian people from coming here. In 1907, for example, the government announced that only those South Asians who travelled directly from India to Canada without their ships stopping in other foreign ports could enter Canada. The government knew

that there was no such route from India to Canada at the time and that this "continuous passage" rule would keep South Asians out.

The rule was challenged by a

group of 376 South Asians who bought passage on a ship called the *Komagata Maru* and sailed directly from India to Vancouver in 1914. Although they had followed the new

Many South Asian men worked in sawmills.

rule, most of the passengers were forbidden to enter Canada. The ship stayed in Vancouver harbour for two months while officials decided what to do. Conditions on board were poor, with very little food or water. In the end, the ship and its passengers were forced back to India.

In the late 1940s and 1950s, immigration laws for South Asians began to relax, and a few more people were allowed to enter Canada. But it wasn't until the 1960s, when racial restrictions in immigration policy were removed, that the number of South Asians coming to Canada really grew.

Karm's Story

Karm Manak's father was one of the first South Asian immigrants. Karm remembers, "It wasn't scary for me seeing a ship for the first time, but I know it was for some other people from our village who came with my dad in 1906. Two of them went back to the village from Calcutta when they saw the ocean and the ship in the harbour. They got frightened ... They thought that it might sink in the water and that would be the end of them … they said we're not going to go on that! So my dad came to Canada and the other two went back to the village."

Canadians of South Asian heritage today:
nearly one million, living in every province and territory. Some are Canadian-born, while others have come recently from India, Pakistan, Bangladesh and Sri Lanka, as well as Africa, Fiji, Mauritius and the Caribbean.

This Sikh temple in Vancouver provided a gathering place for families.

Mrs. Johl's Story

The South Asian immigrants had a strong social network and helped one another get settled in Canada. Mrs. Pritam K. Johl remembers: "In the early days we stuck together through thick and thin. We shared with one another. If someone did not have something then we got together and shared what we had with them. If a newcomer came here we set them up with a place to stay and a job. It was our duty, someone did it for us."

CANADIANS OF SOUTH ASIAN HERITAGE

Shushma Datt is a pioneer in radio and television broadcasting. She started the first South Asian radio station in Canada and is the producer of programs for multicultural television.

Ujjal Dosanjh is a lawyer, politician and long-time human rights activist. He was formerly the Premier of British Columbia, the first South Asian Premier in Canada and a federal Minister of Health.

PRAIRIE SETTLERS

Although immigrants had settled in eastern and western Canada by the 1860s, very few had come to the prairies. There were Scottish settlers in the Red River area and some fur traders. But the land was still mainly the home of the Aboriginal people, who had lived there for thousands of years, and the Métis (people of Aboriginal and European descent).

In spite of this, the Canadian government saw the prairies as a vast, empty wilderness. They decided that settlers and farms were needed and set out to build the Canadian Pacific Railway to bring them. When it was completed, the railway joined eastern Canada to British Columbia and allowed people and goods to easily reach the prairies. The first cross-country trains began running in 1886. Over the next 30 years, the trains brought a flood of settlers to the prairies.

Immigrants travelled to the prairies on special "colonist" trains.

Icelanders

In the 1870s, even before the railway was built, some 1400 immigrants from Iceland arrived in Manitoba. They had suffered many troubles in their home country, such as erupting volcanoes that ruined much of the farmland. The Icelanders settled on the west shore of Lake Winnipeg in a community called New Iceland. They governed themselves, started schools and were self-reliant. But with hardships, such as smallpox, floods and other natural disasters, the population shrank to about 250 in 1881.

Icelandic settlers arrived at New Iceland in 1875.

Canadians of Icelandic heritage today:
about 75 000

Mennonites

About 7000 Mennonites from Russia also settled in southern Manitoba in the 1870s. They had left Russia because of Russian government policies forcing them to do things against their beliefs, such as provide military service. Canada appealed to the Mennonites because the government here offered them land, freedom to follow their own beliefs and a promise they would not have to serve in the army.

Canadians of Mennonite heritage today:
over 200 000

The Last Best West

Clifford Sifton, Canada's Minister of the Interior from 1896 to 1905, believed that the key to a prosperous Canada was attracting immigrant farmers to the Canadian prairies.

Sifton started a powerful promotional campaign to bring farmers from Britain, the United States and Europe to Canada. Pamphlets and posters advertised the prairies as "The Last Best West"

or "The Wondrous West." And the government offered free land to homesteaders — people who would build a home and farm their land for three years.

It worked! From 1900 to 1914, nearly three million people came to the prairies. More than 500 000 were from Europe — mainly south, central and eastern Europe. Nearly one million immigrants were from Britain and another 750 000 were

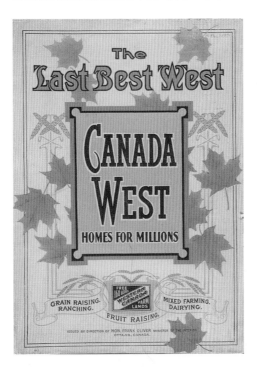

Posters such as this one were used to attract European settlers to the prairies.

Many settlers lived on homesteads where there were few trees, so their first homes were built of sod — pieces of earth and grass cut from the land and stacked in layers.

from the United States. (Many of these were returning Canadians, while others were Scandinavians, Hungarians, Icelanders and Germans who had first gone to the United States.) The prairies filled up, just as the government had hoped.

Many of the early immigrants were shocked by the harsh conditions that awaited them. In winter, they endured cold and blizzards. Summer brought heat, dust storms, prairie fires, drought and swarms of mosquitoes. Families were often far from friends and relatives. Many felt lonely and isolated. Those who didn't speak English often faced discrimination from other settlers.

In spite of the hardships, most settlers stayed on and carved out a new life for themselves and their families. Over time, these hard-working immigrants turned the vast prairie into a rich farming area.

Ukrainian Immigrants

Ukrainians were the largest group of Europeans to arrive on the prairies. From 1891 to 1914, about 170 000 Ukrainians settled here. Many left their homeland because of difficult conditions, including overpopulation, a shortage of good farmland and unfair treatment from their government. They were attracted to the free land in Canada and the opportunity to live in a less restrictive society. Ukrainians often settled close to one another and formed strong community ties. They worked hard to keep their language and culture alive.

Sofie's Story

Sofie Porakyo was three when she came to Canada from Ukraine in 1899. She remembered: "We drove in a wagon from Edmonton to our homestead … my parents and the five children … We children sat huddled on top of the baggage. We … travelled for two days through swampland, along winding roads full of holes … There was a heavy downpour as we were approaching our homestead. We were soaked … [and] hungry …"

But there was no warm home to go to — Sophie's family spent the first winter with another family in a one-room log house. In the spring, they built a shelter, which they shared with another family. It was a tipi made of poplar poles, grass and sod. A piece of carpet was used as a door and saplings covered with hay were used for beds. Later that summer, Sofie's family built their own one-room log cabin.

Polish Immigrants

Another large group to settle on the prairies were Polish immigrants. About 120 000 came to Canada from 1895 to 1913. Some farmed, while others worked in mining or railway construction.

Many of the children of the early Polish settlers later moved to larger cities or towns and opened small businesses.

Canadians of Polish heritage today:
over 800 000, with about half of them living in Ontario

German Immigrants

A large wave of German settlers also came to the prairies. By 1914, about 175 000 Germans lived there. Like other settlers, they worked hard to turn the grasslands into a fertile farming area and create new lives for themselves.

They weren't the only Germans in Canada. Some of the first settlers were German. In fact, by 1867, nearly 200 000 had settled in eastern Canada, mainly in Ontario. Some had come with the Loyalists (at least a third of

Canadians of Ukrainian heritage today:
over one million, with one-third living in Alberta, another third in Ontario and large numbers also in Manitoba, Saskatchewan and British Columbia

Canadians of German heritage today:
nearly three million, with about one million living in Ontario, one-half million in British Columbia and Alberta, and large numbers also in Saskatchewan and Alberta

the Loyalists were German-speaking). Following them came Mennonites from the United States who were attracted to the free land, religious freedom and exemption from military service that Canada offered.

Miriam Toews is an author from Manitoba. She won the Governor General's Award for her book, *A Complicated Kindness*, which tells the story of a teenage girl growing up in a Mennonite community.

Bjarni Tryggvason was born in Iceland in 1945, but came to Canada as a boy. Later, he was chosen as one of Canada's six original astronauts and conducted experiments on the space shuttle *Discovery*.

William Kurelek was a famous artist who painted prairie farm scenes and landscapes inspired by his Ukrainian Canadian heritage. His work includes two children's books, *A Prairie Boy's Summer* and *A Prairie Boy's Winter*.

Wayne Gretzky, nicknamed the "Great One," is a famous hockey player who set or tied almost all of the National Hockey League records. He is the NHL's all-time leading scorer and won four Stanley Cups during his career.

Silken Laumann is an athlete who won many medals for rowing, including an Olympic silver. She was inducted into the Canadian Sports Hall of Fame in 1998. Today, she works with organizations to help refugee children around the world.

BRITISH HOME CHILDREN

In the early 1900s, a Welsh teenager named Ted Taylor sailed to Canada with a group of British children. He was one of about 100 000 children who were sent to Canada between 1869 and the early 1930s. Many were from "homes" (orphanages) in England and so became known as "home children." (In those days, there were great numbers of orphaned and homeless children in London.)

The children came in large groups by ship. Most were between eight and sixteen years old, but some were as young as four. When they got to Canada, they were sent to farms, where boys worked outdoors and girls did household chores. The children had little say in where they went. Brothers and sisters were often separated and sent to different places.

Ted's story was somewhat different. When he got to Canada, he stayed first at a receiving centre (as most home children did) but ran away when he heard stories of boys being mistreated on the farms they'd been sent to. (He later found a job on a horse ranch.)

Life was not easy for the home children. They were expected to work in exchange for a bed and food, a small allowance and the chance to go to school. While some children received these benefits, many did not. Often they were treated like servants. Some were beaten or whipped and deprived of food. They had few options except to run away. Even this was difficult, because the farms were often in isolated areas.

Like many of the home children, Ted Taylor never returned to England. He stayed in Canada, got married and had nine children of his own. Today, descendants of the home children live all across Canada.

The home children thought they would have a better life in Canada. Sadly, this wasn't true for many of them.

Robert's Story

When Robert Clapham was 14, his foster mother died and he was placed in a British orphanage. He came to Canada as a home child in 1929.

He remembers: "The first day after we arrived in Hamilton, the farmers [came] to see about getting a boy to work for them. They took us into a big room and started to look us over … It was just like being at an auction sale, as if they were looking for a prize cow or horse. You … thought you were a slave, no less. I was very homesick … Many nights, I cried myself to sleep … It was a saddening experience leaving England, to go to a strange country, and then having the farmer's children make fun of you … I will never forget as long as I live."

Dr. Barnardo

Thomas Barnardo, trained as a doctor and missionary, dedicated his life to helping homeless children in London in the late 1800s. Hoping to

give them a new start, he sent some 30 000 children to Canada. They were called Barnardo Boys and Girls. (As well as Barnardo, other people and organizations also sent home children to Canada.) Barnardo believed that the children would be better off away from the poverty of England and would benefit from the clean air, hard work and discipline of Canada. Sadly, this was not the case for many of them.

The practice of sending home children to Canada ended in the

A farmer chose the home boy he wanted to work on his farm. The boy had no say in where he went.

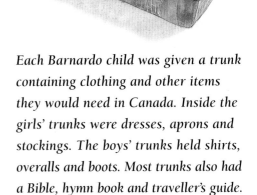

Each Barnardo child was given a trunk containing clothing and other items they would need in Canada. Inside the girls' trunks were dresses, aprons and stockings. The boys' trunks held shirts, overalls and boots. Most trunks also had a Bible, hymn book and traveller's guide.

1930s. People became critical of taking children from their home country and using them as poorly paid workers in another.

PIER 21

In the mid-1900s, newcomers from Europe and Britain travelled to Canada by ship across the Atlantic Ocean, just as earlier immigrants had done. Fortunately, the ships — and the journey — were much more comfortable by then.

From 1928 to 1971, many ships docked at Pier 21 in Halifax, the main harbour for immigrants. More than one million people entered Canada through this historic gateway. (Other ships also landed at Montreal, Vancouver and St. John's.)

Pier 21 was closed in 1971 when ship immigration from Europe slowed and immigrants began arriving in Canada by plane. Today, Pier 21 is a museum that commemorates the many brave immigrants who passed through its doors.

Arriving at Pier 21

What was it like to be a new immigrant arriving at Pier 21 in the early years? First, you gathered up your hand baggage and walked along a gangplank from the ship to the dock. You waited while your heavy baggage was unloaded and inspected (to prevent certain foods, plants or other illegal items from being brought into Canada).

From there, you walked to a reception area where you were examined by a doctor (or other medical staff) and interviewed by an immigration official.

The doctor looked for serious diseases or other health problems. If you were sick, you were quarantined (kept in a medical treatment area) or sent back to your home country. Sometimes, one person in a family was sent back, while the rest were allowed to stay.

Next, you waited for your turn to meet with an immigration official who decided whether or not you could stay in Canada. Your passport and other documents were checked, and you were asked questions, such as: Where are you from?

Newcomers waited in this assembly hall for their turn to be interviewed. The room was crowded with people and the sounds of many languages.

Where are you going? How much money do you have? Can you read or write? People who didn't speak English were helped by an interpreter.

If your medical examination and immigration interview went well, you were allowed to stay in Canada. (Those with a criminal past were returned to Europe.) A welcome committee of volunteers from the Red Cross, Sisters of Service or Jewish Immigrant Aid Society greeted you. They offered comforting words, food and a place to sleep. They also cared for babies and small children whose parents were exhausted by the journey. Priests gave spiritual help to anyone who wished it.

From Pier 21, many people boarded special "colonist" trains for other parts of the country. Life in Canada had begun!

Kaarina's Story

Kaarina Brooks was nine when she came to Canada from Finland in 1951. She wrote in her diary: "We got off the boat and now we are all sitting in a huge hall at Pier 21. It's filled with rows and rows of benches like a church, only it's much bigger and not at all pretty … It's all crowded with people and everyone is just sitting and sitting, waiting to be called up to talk to one of the men who are at the front of the room, behind a long desk. They sure are slow!

Antonio's Story

Antonio Saez Jiménez, who arrived from Spain in 1958, said, "I remember well the ladies who came to me asking if I needed any help. I could see them helping people, old and young, taking care of babies and trying to communicate with so many Greeks and Italians who could not speak English or French. They really did do a magnificent job!"

THE WAR YEARS

When World War I broke out in 1914, immigration to Canada came almost to a stop. People began to fear the immigrants who had come from countries Canada was fighting with. These immigrants were called "enemy aliens" and were treated harshly. They were fired from their jobs, placed under police watch and about 8000 were sent to internment (prison) camps. Their churches and language schools were closed. People of German descent and immigrants from the Austro-Hungarian Empire (including Hungarian, Ukrainian, Polish, Romanian and Czech people) suffered the most.

After the war, the government stopped accepting immigrants based on their ability to contribute to the economy. Instead, only immigrants from certain countries were allowed in.

The most desirable immigrants were those from Britain and the United States, followed by northern and western Europeans. People from other parts of Europe were less desirable, which meant they were allowed to come to Canada only to do farm work or labouring jobs, such as railway building. South Europeans and Jews were generally refused entry, as were Asian and Black people.

Immigration slowed, especially in the 1930s, during the Great Depression. The Depression left many people without work, and some Canadians feared that immigrants would compete for the remaining jobs. So very few immigrants were allowed into Canada. In fact, nearly 30 000 immigrants who had come earlier were deported (sent back to their home countries).

These German Canadians were sent to an internment camp during World War I.

Ideal Settlers

This was the list of preferred immigrants according to Canadian immigration authorities of the time. The most preferred immigrants are at the top of the list, and the least preferred are at the bottom.

British and Americans
French
Belgians
Dutch
Scandinavians
Swiss
Finns
Russians
Austro-Hungarians
Germans
Ukrainians
Poles
Italians
South Slavs
Greeks
Syrians
Jews
Asians
Gypsies
Blacks

Signs such as this one were posted to keep Jews out of swimming areas and other public places in the 1920s and 1930s.

Hostility toward immigrants arose again when World War II broke out in 1939. During this war, Japanese people were taken from their homes and sent to live in relocation camps (see pages 28-29). Italian immigrants lost their jobs, had their stores vandalized and many rights taken away. Hundreds of them were sent to internment camps. Some German immigrants were also interned.

Turned Away!

By the mid-1920s, most Jews were barred entry into Canada, as a result of immigration restrictions.

In 1939, the ship *S.S. St. Louis* carrying Jewish refugees set sail from Germany to Cuba. (Refugees are people fleeing danger in their own country and looking for safety in another.) The refugees were desperate to escape Nazi persecution and death in Germany, but Cuba refused them entry.

A newspaper article of the time stated, "Women wept and children tugged at their mothers' hands in bewilderment. Many of the 918 Jews appeared to have abandoned hope … Four refugees attempted to take their lives after learning of the order forbidding them to land."

The refugees appealed to other countries, including Argentina, Uruguay, Paraguay, the United States and Canada. None would let them in. The ship was forced to return to Europe, where most of the passengers later died in concentration camps.

Why did Canada refuse entry to the Jewish refugees? Anti-Semitism (discrimination directed at people of Jewish descent) was common in Canada in the 1920s, 1930s and 1940s. Jews were barred from many public places and some jobs. Some landlords would not sell or rent homes to them, and universities often discriminated against Jewish students.

Jewish refugees were refused entry to Canada in the 1930s and 1940s when they needed a safe haven the most. A Canadian government official of the time was asked how many Jews Canada would be willing to admit. He replied, "None is too many."

The people on this ship could have been saved if Canada had opened its doors to them.

GUEST CHILDREN

Bombs were exploding over London during World War II, and families cowered for safety in air-raid shelters. Terrified parents decided to send their children — some as young as five years old — to Canada for their protection.

About 7000 British children came to Canada in the early years of World War II. They were called "guest children" because they would be guests in Canada until the war ended.

Once here, guest children were cared for by relatives or foster families for up to five years. They went to school, made friends and adjusted to a Canadian way of life. Many became attached to their caregivers and found it hard to leave when the war ended. Some children liked Canada so much that they came back as adults to live here permanently.

Guest children stopped coming to Canada after a ship carrying about 90 of them was sunk by a German torpedo in 1940. Seventy-seven children and their adult caretakers died. Parents now believed it was too dangerous to send their children across the Atlantic.

Hazel's Story
Hazel Wilson was 14 when she came as a guest child in 1940. She went to Winnipeg and lived with a couple who had no children of their own. At first, Hazel was lonely. But over time, she became close to her foster parents. She joined Girl Guides, took piano lessons and made friends.

Hazel kept in touch with her English family through letters. When she returned to England in 1944, she was thrilled to see them — but missed her Canadian friends and foster parents very much. In 1947, Hazel moved back to Canada. The rest of her family soon followed and were all living here by 1955.

About 3000 guest children passed through Pier 21. Each brought a small suitcase filled with clothes and personal belongings. Young children brought dolls or teddy bears to keep them company.

WAR BRIDES

After World War II, thousands of women who had married Canadian soldiers in Britain and Europe came to Canada. The women were called war brides. By the end of 1946, nearly 50 000 women and their 22 000 children had arrived. They were the largest group of immigrants to come to Canada since the Great Depression of the 1930s.

Most of the war brides were British, but some also came from Belgium, France, Holland and Italy. These women left their countries and families to begin a new life with their husbands in Canada.

Like other newcomers, many war brides felt homesick. And not all were welcomed by their husbands' families. Some women who had come from cities in Britain and Europe ended up in farming areas and found it difficult to adjust to rural life. Others spoke no English and had to quickly learn the language. In spite of these challenges, most war brides adapted to the country, raised families and stayed in Canada permanently.

Hilda's Story

Hilda Bradshaw came from London as a war bride in 1946. She went to live in Carrot River, Saskatchewan, with her husband. They drove to their farm with her in-laws along a narrow dirt road with thick brush on either side. Hilda's father-in-law said, "Let's get her home tonight … because if she sees Carrot River in the daylight, she will go back right away."

Hilda said, "We laughed about that years later. However, I did stay and learned to do everything a farm wife was supposed to do: canning, breadmaking, pies and cakes, making butter and all the rest of it. I learned a lot and people were so helpful."

Many war brides brought young children, which made a long trip even more difficult. Everyone battled seasickness. There were no proper diaper-changing or bathing areas on the ships and trains. And the children often grew restless.

JEWISH WAR ORPHANS

World War II was a terrible time for Jews. Six million were put to death in Europe by the Nazis. This period came to be known as the Holocaust. Those who could, tried to escape and asked to be admitted to other countries where they could be safe. Everywhere, they found the doors closed to them. Canada admitted fewer than 5000 Jews. Some say it had the worst record of any country that provided refuge.

After the war, from 1947 to 1949, Canada accepted 1123 Jewish war orphans as part of the War Orphans Project. The project was organized by the Canadian Jewish community and approved by the government.

The children who came to Canada had lost their parents in the Holocaust and had survived in concentration camps or by hiding. They were allowed to come to Canada if Jewish Canadians agreed to take them into their homes and care for them.

The children travelled on ships across the Atlantic, then boarded trains to places across Canada. They were met at the stations by Jewish families who took them in.

Jewish Immigration in the Early Years

The first Jewish immigrants came to Canada in 1760. By 1851, there were about 450 Jews here. Most lived in Montreal and played an important role in the economy, industry and business.

Over the next 90 years, nearly 200 000 Jewish immigrants came to Canada — but that stopped in World War II. Many Jews might have been saved had Canada opened its doors (see page 41). After the war, restrictions against Jewish immigration began to relax. About 135 000 Jews came to Canada between the end of World War II and the 1980s.

Robbie's Story

Robbie Waisman was one of the orphans. He spent much of the war in Buchenwald, a concentration camp where many Jewish prisoners were punished, starved and put to death. When the war ended, Robbie was freed from the camp. He learned that he and his sister were the only members of their family who had survived.

Robbie came to Canada as a war orphan in 1948. He was 17 years old. From Halifax, he rode the train to Calgary to begin a new life with the Goresht family. The Goreshts treated Robbie like a valued family member. He quickly found work and, before long, became an accountant. Later, he owned and operated a children's clothing store, got married and had two children of his own.

Today, Robbie Waisman is president of the Vancouver Holocaust Education Centre. "When I speak to

Robbie, after he was freed from Buchenwald

young people about my experiences during the Holocaust, I always ask them to keep an open mind when they see and meet newcomers to this country," he says. "I ask them to experience the adventure of getting to know other kinds of people. Each one of us possesses unique and wonderful qualities, regardless of colour or religion."

Like Robbie Waisman, many of the Jewish war orphans stayed in Canada permanently. They made close and long-lasting attachments with the families who took them in and became valuable members of Canadian society.

Canadians of Jewish heritage today:
about 330 000 people of Jewish descent, with nearly 200 000 in Ontario and 90 000 in Quebec

---

CANADIANS OF JEWISH HERITAGE

Karen Levine is an award-winning CBC producer and children's author. Her book *Hana's Suitcase* tells the true story of Hana Brady, a girl who lost her life in the Holocaust, and how children remember Hana today.

Stephen Lewis is a humanitarian and former politician. He received the Order of Canada for working to improve the lives of less fortunate people around the world. He is also the former Canadian ambassador to the United Nations.

Moses Znaimer is the founder and producer of many independent television stations, including MuchMusic and Bravo. He has received many honours for his work in promoting ethnic diversity and racial tolerance.

DISPLACED PERSONS AND REFUGEES

After World War II, there was a refugee crisis in Europe. Many Europeans were homeless and jobless. In Canada, there was a labour shortage, so the government began looking to Europe for workers. Public opinion about immigrants had started to shift and some Canadians were calling for more flexible immigration laws.

In the 10 years following World War II, over one million immigrants were admitted to Canada. They were Polish, Ukrainian, Hungarian, German, Austrian, Jewish, Latvian, Serbian, Croatian, Italian, Czech, Dutch and Russian. These immigrants came seeking a new country and a new life after the hard years of war in Europe.

A large number were refugees, now called Displaced Persons (DPs) — a term that came into use after the war. Many found themselves outside their home countries after the war and could not return. Some had spent years in concentration or labour camps.

Canada was one of the first countries in the world to admit displaced persons. Nearly 250 000 came to Canada between 1947 and 1962. Many had their journeys paid (or partially paid) by the Canadian government.

The refugees often came with little more than the clothes they were wearing. Some had no money, passports, birth certificates or sponsors (people to support them as they settled in Canada). Most were frightened and shaken by their war experiences.

The newcomers faced many challenges. They had to adjust to a new country, learn a new language, find jobs and care for their uprooted families. Many had to wait a long time to be accepted by other Canadians.

Ausma Levalds was eight years old when she and her family came to Canada from Latvia in 1949. She was honoured as the 50 000th displaced person to arrive at Pier 21.

Voyage on the *Sarabande*

Some people were so desperate to leave Europe that they came to Canada in small boats not meant for ocean crossings. On August 19, 1949, the *Sarabande* arrived in Halifax carrying 238 displaced persons. Sixty of them were children. The passengers were from Poland, Estonia, Latvia and Finland. Their month at sea had been rough and dangerous, with little food or water. Many wore numbers that had been tattooed on them in the concentration camps. Fortunately, Canada's doors were now open to refugees, and they safely entered the country.

Anna's Story

Anna Kerz was born in 1947 in an Austrian camp for displaced persons. (Her parents had to leave their homeland, Yugoslavia, because of the war.) People lived in rustic buildings, grew their own food and got water from a central tap.

Anna remembers: "When I was born, bombs no longer came whistling out of the sky … A truce had been declared and treaties signed. But there is a huge difference between the end of fighting and the beginning of peace. Especially a peace that puts food on the table, reunites your family, lets you find work and a home. Peace takes time. And that is how I came to spend the early years of my life in a DP camp. DP stands for Displaced Person … it means you have no home to go back to."

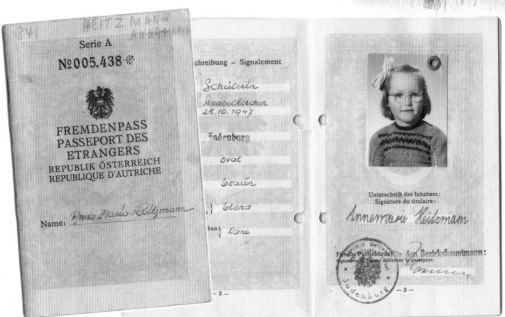

This is Anna's passport — the document she used to enter Canada.

In 1954, Anna and her parents left the camp and sailed to Canada. She said, "It was easy to see what we were leaving behind; almost everything we owned and every single person we knew. The hard part was deciding what to take along. What do you take when all your belongings have to fit into one old wooden trunk?"

Although leaving Europe was difficult, Anna and her parents settled in Toronto and made a new home for themselves.

POST-WAR IMMIGRANTS

Along with the displaced persons were many other immigrants. A large number of them were German, Italian and Dutch. To the people who had endured years of war in Europe, Canada looked like a safe and inviting nation. And the Canadian government wanted immigrants — Canada's economy was booming and workers were needed. From 1946 to 1965, two and a half million people came to Canada. (They are called post-war immigrants because they arrived after the war.)

The government still preferred immigrants from Britain, the United States and Western Europe, but they were willing to take people from other countries as well. For example, immigrants who had earlier been unwelcome were now allowed into Canada. But the prime minister at the time, William Lyon Mackenzie King, told Canadians that while immigration would help Canada grow, immigrants would be carefully selected so as not to change the character of the country.

Many of the post-war immigrants came well-equipped to start a new life here. They had job skills or professions and some had money to set up homes for themselves.

Dutch Immigrants

In Holland, much of the good farmland had been destroyed or flooded during the war and farmers could no longer make a living. In Canada, many farmers were leaving their farms to work in the cities. So, the Canadian and Dutch governments sponsored Dutch farmers to move to Canada and take up farming here. About 170 000 Dutch immigrants arrived from 1946 to 1965.

Not all of the Dutch immigrants were farmers. Dutch professionals and skilled workers also came at this time.

Maurice's Story

Maurice Verkaar was a baby when he came to Canada in 1953. His parents were eager to leave Europe because they felt there wasn't much of a future for young families in post-war Holland. The family sold most of its belongings and packed the rest into two suitcases. They travelled by ship to Montreal, then by train to Winnipeg.

As a new Canadian, Maurice didn't feel like an outsider. He said, "We lived in the west end of Winnipeg and almost all of my friends had parents with accents. My parents were happy and anxious to become Canadians."

Canadians of Dutch heritage today:
nearly one million, with almost half living in Ontario

Toronto is a city of ethnically diverse neighbourhoods. This is an Italian section of the city.

Italian Immigrants

From 1946 to 1965, nearly 400 000 Italian immigrants came to Canada. The Canadian government and private companies helped sponsor many of them.

Most Italians settled in the cities, especially Toronto and Montreal. Many of the men worked in construction and building trades, while the women often worked in clothing factories.

Other Italian immigrants ran food-making businesses, fruit markets, bakeries and restaurants. They introduced Canadians to pasta and pizza, some of our most popular foods today.

Canadians of Italian heritage today:

about 1.3 million, with nearly 800 000 living in Ontario. This is one of the largest populations of Italians outside of Italy.

CANADIAN OF DUTCH HERITAGE

Roméo Dallaire is a retired Lieutenant General who had a distinguished career in the Canadian Forces for over 30 years. He commanded the United Nations Peacekeeping Force to Rwanda during a civil war there and received the Order of Canada for his courage and leadership. Today, he works on behalf of war-affected children.

CANADIAN OF ITALIAN HERITAGE

Mario Bernardi is an internationally renowned musician and conductor. He has won many major awards, including two Governor General's awards, and is regarded as the leading conductor of his generation. He received the Order of Canada for forming the National Arts Centre Orchestra. Today, he is principal conductor for the CBC Radio Orchestra.

CHANGING TIMES

By 1960, nearly 18 million people lived in Canada. And immigrants were still arriving. From 1956 to 1967, more than one and a half million immigrants came to Canada, mostly from Europe.

The new immigration laws said that no one could be excluded from Canada because of race, religion or place of birth. This was very different from the earlier system of selection that discriminated against people of certain races or countries. The new regulations now looked at the education, training and skills of immigrants as the main requirements for coming to Canada. People would be admitted based on their ability to contribute to Canada's economy.

This change led to a big increase in immigration to Canada. Large numbers of immigrants began arriving from Asia and the Caribbean. By the early 1970s, people from Asia and other non-European countries made up more than half of all immigrants to Canada. This trend has continued ever since.

Caribbean Immigrants

After the immigration laws were changed, about 64 000 people from the Caribbean, also called the West Indies, came to Canada. (The Caribbean includes island countries, such as Barbados, Jamaica, Trinidad and Haiti.) Most of the newcomers settled in Ontario and Quebec. Nearly one-third of them worked in professional and technical jobs. In the 1970s and 1980s, another 315 000 Caribbean immigrants arrived.

In 1962, the immigration laws were dramatically changed. Pressure from well-established immigrants and a growing feeling that discrimination was wrong may have helped bring about the change.

Every summer, Toronto hosts Caribana — the largest Caribbean festival in North America. Caribana began in 1967. The celebration was a sign of Canada's growing multicultural mix. This is the Caribana parade today.

Rosemary's Story

Rosemary Brown was a politician, social worker, activist, professor, feminist and a member of the Order of Canada. She worked tirelessly to achieve equality and social justice for women and minority groups. Rosemary was the first Black woman to be elected to political office in Canada as a Member of the Legislative Assembly of British Columbia. She also ran for the leadership of a federal political party.

Rosemary came to Canada from Jamaica in 1950 to attend university. It was here she first encountered racism. Other students wouldn't share a room or eat meals with her because of the colour of her skin.

Later, she found it hard to get a job or rent a house, and no one would sit beside her on the bus.

Rather than stopping Rosemary, these events encouraged her to fight

for equality. She once said, "To be Black and female in a society which is both racist and sexist is to be in a unique position of having no place to go but up." Rosemary was active in social causes until her death in 2003, at age 72.

Canadians of Caribbean heritage today:
about 500 000, with almost 350 000 in Ontario and 100 000 in Quebec

CANADIANS OF CARIBBEAN HERITAGE

Michaëlle Jean is the first Black Governor General of Canada and an award-winning journalist, broadcaster, filmmaker and social activist. She is an advocate for young people and the disadvantaged. Michaëlle's family fled to Canada from Haiti in 1968 to escape the violent Haitian government of the time.

Oscar Peterson is one of the world's best jazz pianists and composers. He has won many awards for his music, including Junos, Grammys and a Genie. He has also been awarded the Order of Canada for his enormous contribution to music.

Hungarian and Czech Refugees

Canada became a haven for refugees. In 1956, Canada took in about 37 000 refugees who were fleeing communist Hungary after a failed uprising. Hungarian citizens, who had been demonstrating in the streets for a more liberal government, were overpowered by soldiers and tanks from the USSR (now Russia). Hundreds of Hungarians were killed and many more were jailed. Nearly 200 000 fled the country. Canada set aside its normal immigration rules in order to help the refugees as quickly as possible.

Another 11 000 Czech refugees came to Canada in 1968 when the USSR took control of their country. Most of the refugees were highly skilled people who quickly adapted to Canadian society. (Other Hungarian and Czech immigrants had come to Canada in earlier times.)

After Soviet tanks rolled into Prague, Czechoslovakia, in 1968, Canada welcomed thousands of Czech refugees.

CANADIAN OF HUNGARIAN HERITAGE

Alanis Morissette is an internationally known singer-songwriter. She has sold more than 40 million records worldwide and won Juno and Grammy awards. Her mother is Hungarian and her father is French Canadian.

Canadians of Hungarian heritage today:
about 270 000

CANADIAN OF CZECH HERITAGE

Thomas Bata was the owner of Bata Shoes, the largest shoe manufacturing company in the world. The company has nearly 5000 stores and factories in 60 countries. It has sold more than 40 billion pairs of shoes worldwide.

Canadians of Czech heritage today:
about 80 000

American War Resisters

Beginning in 1965 and lasting until the early 1970s, thousands of young men from the United States, commonly called "draft dodgers," came to Canada. They came because they didn't agree with the Vietnam War and did not want to fight in it. So they left their country in protest and "dodged" (avoided) the military draft that would force them to serve. No one knows the exact number of war resisters who came — it may be as high as 40 000 (a number that includes family members who came with them). Many other American immigrants came to Canada before the war resisters.

Ugandan Refugees

During the early 1900s, many Asians moved to Uganda (and other parts of Africa) where some eventually became shopkeepers and professionals.

In 1972, Uganda's president Idi Amin gave all Asian Ugandans 90 days to leave the country. Fearing for their lives and safety, tens of thousands of people fled to other countries, leaving their homes and businesses behind. Canada accepted 7000 refugees. Many of them were highly trained and educated people.

The Canadian government organized an emergency airlift by chartering planes to fly the refugees from Uganda to Canada. A Canadian immigration team also went to Uganda to speed up the immigration process.

Rahim's Story

Rahim Jaffer was a nine-month-old baby when he and his parents fled Uganda for Canada with only a diaper bag and a suitcase. They were forced to leave their home, business and everything else behind. Soldiers were visible on the streets, and stories of people being attacked or killed were circulating.

The family knew they had to leave Uganda to stay safe.

Rahim grew up in Canada and was elected as a Member of Parliament in 1997, at age 25. During a debate in the House of Commons, Rahim said, "My family's experience was that they lost everything through the process of coming to Canada. The only saving grace was that we came to a country that welcomed us with open arms and gave us an opportunity to make a new start." Today, Rahim's family owns and operates a bakery in Edmonton.

The Ugandan refugees came by plane instead of by ship as earlier immigrants had done.

CANADIAN OF ASIAN UGANDAN HERITAGE

Mobina Jaffer is a lawyer and the first South Asian, first African and first Muslim woman to be appointed to the Senate. She is an advocate for human rights issues, especially in seeking equality and justice for women of colour.

CANADA OPENS ITS DOORS

By the 1980s, people of many languages, customs, faiths and colours were a permanent part of Canadian society. A vibrant multicultural Canada was emerging, and more immigrants were arriving to add to the mix.

A new Immigration Act in 1976 helped further open the doors to immigrants. The act set out goals for reuniting families, being fair to immigrants of all races, providing safety to refugees and helping newcomers adjust to Canada.

This South Asian shopping district in Vancouver is just one of Canada's many neighbourhoods that expresses a rich culture and heritage.

More than two and a half million immigrants arrived during the 1970s and 1980s. Most came from Africa, Central and South America, the Caribbean and the Middle East. By 1986, nearly 40 percent of immigrants were from Asia. The newcomers settled mainly in Toronto, Vancouver and Montreal.

In 1971, Prime Minister Pierre Trudeau announced a new policy of multiculturalism. He said the government would support and encourage Canada's diverse ethnic groups "to share their cultural expression and values with other Canadians and so contribute to a richer life for us all."

Chilean and Latin American Refugees

In 1973, the Chilean army overthrew the democratically elected government of Chile. People who had supported the old government were in danger of being arrested, imprisoned, tortured or even killed by the forces of the new one. The Canadian government was reluctant to admit the refugees, but organizations such as Amnesty International, as well as church, labour and Latino groups, pressured the government. Some 7000 refugees were allowed in. (Other Latin American immigrants also came to Canada during the 1970s and later.)

> **Canadians of Latin American heritage today:**
> more than 200 000

Vietnamese "Boat People"

In 1975, when the Vietnam War ended, over one million people fled Vietnam, Cambodia and Laos. From 1979 to 1980, Canada took in some 70 000 refugees from these countries.

Many of the refugees risked their lives in crowded, leaky boats to leave their homelands and ended up in refugee camps in Thailand and Malaysia. These refugees, known as "boat people," faced terrors such as typhoons, sinking ships and violent pirate attacks at sea. Many Canadians helped sponsor the refugees, allowing a large number to come to Canada.

Hieu's Story

Hieu Tran came to Canada as a teenager in 1981. He said, "Millions of Vietnamese tried to escape [after the fall of Saigon] by boats or by land … Hundreds of thousands of people died because of … thirst, hunger, pirates in the ocean … getting lost in the forests, being killed by wild animals or shot down by soldiers. I was one of the boat people."

After escaping from a labour camp, Hieu boarded a small wooden boat with 46 other people. They floated in the ocean for three days before being rescued and taken to a refugee camp in Singapore. Hieu's brother, who had arrived in Canada in 1980, sponsored Hieu so that he, too, could come to Canada. Hieu said, "In Canada … I have the freedom to think, speak, read, associate … That is what I escaped for."

> **Canadians of Vietnamese heritage today:**
> about 150 000

The Nansen Medal

In 1986, the United Nations High Commissioner for Refugees awarded the Nansen Medal to Canada for its work in helping refugees. Canada had taken in more than 150 000 refugees in the previous 10 years.

MODERN TIMES

In the last 25 years, more than three million immigrants from all parts of the world have arrived in Canada, making it a truly multicultural country.

People describe Canada as a "mosaic" of different cultures. (A mosaic is a picture made with small pieces of differently coloured glass or stone set together.) They say Canada is a place where people from a mix of backgrounds and many nations can live as Canadians, while keeping their own heritage alive.

The signs of the mosaic are everywhere in Canada — from the rich variety of languages to diverse styles of clothing, restaurants, radio stations, newspapers, businesses and places of worship. New Canadians, as well as those born here, are free to observe their customs and traditions in a country that encourages people to be proud of their ethnic heritage.

Canada's largest cities are home to people of many diverse backgrounds.

Newcomers Today

Immigration has made Canada a vibrant and interesting country. People from more than 200 ethnic groups now call Canada home.

Today, nearly 60 percent of immigrants arrive from Asia (including the Middle East). Smaller numbers are also from the Caribbean, Africa, Central and South America, Europe and the United States. Most people come to join family members in Canada, find work or start businesses.

About 200 000 immigrants arrive each year. Of these, some 20 000 are refugees. The newcomers settle mainly in Canada's largest cities. One in five students in Toronto and Vancouver is a new Canadian.

Kosovar Refugees

In the late 1980s, the Canadian government was worried that some refugees were making false claims to enter the country, so the rules for admission were tightened up. But certain refugees were still accepted. For example, in 1999, when violent conditions arose in Kosovo (Europe), ethnic Albanian people feared for their lives. Nearly a million citizens were displaced from their homes and needed a safe place to go. Canada provided emergency evacuation flights from Europe. The government, churches and community groups helped some 7000 refugees find a safe haven here.

Refugees or Illegal Immigrants?

Refugees are people who have a well-founded fear of persecution in their homeland. Thousands are admitted to Canada every year. When people who are not true refugees try to enter Canada, they are usually denied entry. For example, in 1999, nearly 600 people from China arrived

The refugees from Kosovo had lost everything and were shaken by their experiences in Europe. Red Cross volunteers gave teddy bears to the children to welcome them to Canada.

on the coast of British Columbia. They had spent two months at sea crowded into four old cargo ships, with very little food or water. The group included 39 children, some as young as 11 years old. The people hadn't applied to enter Canada as immigrants and they didn't qualify as refugees — but they still hoped they could stay. Instead, they were declared "illegal immigrants" and put in jail, while officials decided what to do. Most were sent back to China.

Racism

While many Canadians believe that being a multicultural country makes Canada a better place, not everyone shares this view. Racism — the unfair treatment of people based on their race — is an issue that many Canadians faced in the past and continue to face today. Schools, churches and community leaders are working hard to put a stop to this hurtful practice.

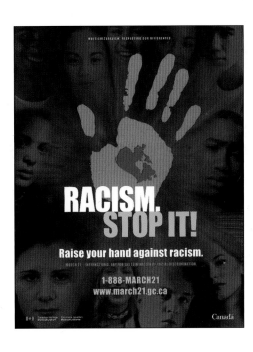

ALICIA'S STORY

About 200 000 immigrants come to Canada every year. Each one of them has a story. This is Alicia's story.

Alicia was born in El Salvador and came to Canada when she was four. Today, she is 17 and lives in a Vancouver suburb. She says, "We left El Salvador because of the war. My parents decided that going to another country was best for our family. There was a Canadian program that took in people from countries in crisis and that's how we came to be here."

Alicia came with her parents, a baby brother and two-year-old sister. (Alicia now has another sister who was born in Canada.) The family flew from El Salvador to Toronto, where immigration officials admitted them to Canada. Then they boarded a plane for Vancouver.

Getting Settled

Alicia's family first stayed at Vancouver's Welcome House, which provides short-term, low-cost housing for new immigrants. Welcome House is part of the Immigrant Services Society, an organization that helps newcomers settle into Canada and learn about banking, shopping, transportation and jobs. It also has translators and interpreters.

After a month, Alicia's family moved to their own apartment. Alicia started kindergarten and went to ESL classes to learn English. She says, "I remember having difficulties talking to the other kids because of the language barrier. But I learned English easily and soon made my first best friend."

Facing Challenges

Alicia says, "I've never experienced direct discrimination, but I have experienced it indirectly, through my parents. They have traces of accents and have sometimes been looked down upon for their backgrounds. It hurts me very much to see this.

"Whenever I see racism, it upsets me. Everyone at some time has been 'new' or 'different,' so it's not fair to bully, ignore or look down on someone who can't express him- or herself in a different language."

Alicia's parents both graduated with engineering degrees in El Salvador. But they haven't been able to work in their fields here because Canada doesn't recognize their qualifications. Many immigrants face this problem and often earn less than they would in their chosen careers.

Alicia and her family arriving in Canada.

58

Alicia's Citizenship Ceremony

Four years after they arrived in Canada, Alicia's parents applied to become Canadian citizens. They had to take a test and answer questions about Canada and were relieved and happy when they passed it.

Alicia remembers the day of her citizenship ceremony. "My mum dressed us up in our Sunday best. We sang *O Canada* with lots of other people and got little pins with the Canadian flag on them. My parents were joyful to officially become Canadian citizens."

Becoming a Canadian Citizen

If you were born in another country and want to become a Canadian citizen, you need to apply for citizenship.

To apply, you must:
- be 18 years or older (parents can apply for their children)
- speak English or French
- be a permanent resident (legally permitted to live in Canada)
- have lived in Canada for three out of the previous four years
- pass a test with questions about Canada

Finally, you are invited to a citizenship ceremony where you take an oath of citizenship. You are presented with a Certificate of Canadian Citizenship and then everyone sings *O Canada*.

Congratulations! You are now a Canadian citizen.

Alicia's Message

"I want to tell all the new Canadian kids and families out there to keep going, no matter how hard it gets. *Todo pasa pro una razon* — everything happens for a reason. Just keep hope and know there is always a bright side and things will only get better."

She also says, "In Canada we are all blessed. I am thankful for everything I have and everything Canada has to offer."

COMING TO CANADA TODAY

What's it like to come to Canada as an immigrant today? It's exciting and frightening, all at the same time. Many newcomers say that Canada is a good place, but that it's hard to adjust to a new country. They miss the family and friends they left behind. The language here can be different, the weather may be colder and they too often face discrimination.

For those who have come from war-torn countries or refugee camps, Canada offers safety and a chance for a life free from violence, hunger and suffering. But the adjustment to a new country is still not easy.

Here's what some new Canadian kids, from a school near Vancouver, have to say about coming to Canada.

Amir, 13, Iran

When I came here, I didn't know English and I had no friends. It was very complicating. We had visited Canada before and we loved it. It was like heaven compared to Iran. The worst thing about Canada is the racism against African Americans. I love Canada. I am Canadian!

Alissa, 13, Russia

I thought that everything in Canada would be different — like coming to a new planet or something, but when I walked off the plane, it wasn't so different. I was surprised that there were so many new people coming to Canada like me.

Amir   *Alissa*   *Tim*   *Cecilia*

Tim, 12, Africa

I came from Africa when I was 10. A friend had told my dad all about Canada. I remember stressing because it took so long to get here. The best thing about Canada are the free schools. The worst is the junk food.

Cecilia, 12, Chile

We came to Canada because my mom's family lived here. I also had a disease called croup in Chile because of the smog there. In Canada, the air is so clean! But, even though I've lived here for nine years, I still don't feel like I belong.

Daniel, 13, Philippines

We came to Canada for a better future and more opportunity. I remember riding an airplane to Canada and my uncle picking us up at the airport. I was surprised that Canada had so many immigrants.

Stacey, 11, Ukraine

It was pretty scary and exciting when I came to Canada. I was also sad because I had to leave all my friends behind.

Lee, 11, South Korea

I rode an airplane and it took a very long time to get to Canada. We came here for my education. My friends are kind but I miss my dad very much.

Stephanie, 14, China

Moving here has been the best experience. I have made tons of friends. Canada has influenced me in a way that I shall never forget. Thanks, Canada, you made a difference in me!

Daniel *Stacey* *Lee* *Stephanie*

IMMIGRATION FACTS AND FIGURES

Canada's Cultural Mix

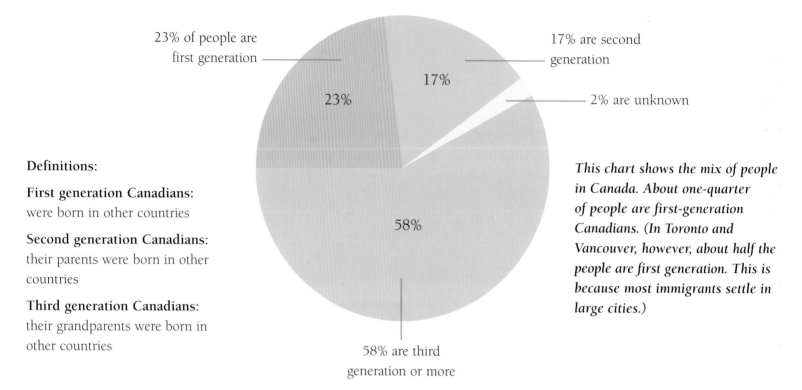

23% of people are first generation — 23%

17% are second generation — 17%

2% are unknown

58% are third generation or more — 58%

Definitions:

First generation Canadians: were born in other countries

Second generation Canadians: their parents were born in other countries

Third generation Canadians: their grandparents were born in other countries

This chart shows the mix of people in Canada. About one-quarter of people are first-generation Canadians. (In Toronto and Vancouver, however, about half the people are first generation. This is because most immigrants settle in large cities.)

Top Ten Countries for Immigration to Canada

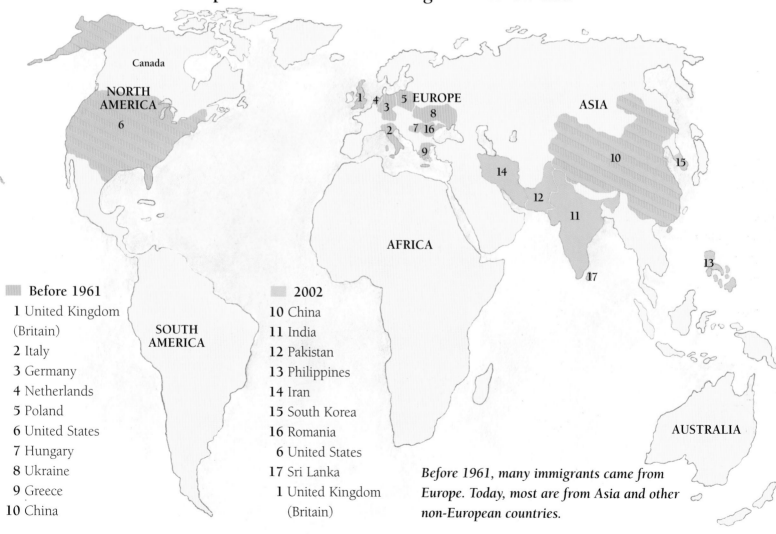

Before 1961

1 United Kingdom (Britain)
2 Italy
3 Germany
4 Netherlands
5 Poland
6 United States
7 Hungary
8 Ukraine
9 Greece
10 China

2002

10 China
11 India
12 Pakistan
13 Philippines
14 Iran
15 South Korea
16 Romania
6 United States
17 Sri Lanka
1 United Kingdom (Britain)

Before 1961, many immigrants came from Europe. Today, most are from Asia and other non-European countries.

IMMIGRATION WORDS

Aboriginal person: someone who is descended from the first people in Canada

ancestor: someone, such as a parent, grandparent or great-grandparent, whom a person is descended from

boat person: someone who flees his or her country in a boat

Cabinet Minister: an elected official who is head of a government department, such as finance or health

Canadian citizen: a person who has all rights and privileges under Canadian law, including the right to vote

colony: a settlement in one country that is ruled by the government in another

descendant: someone, such as a child, grandchild or great-grandchild, who is born into a certain family or group

displaced person: someone forced out of his or her country by war, famine or other terrible event; a refugee

ethnic background: the shared race, nationality, language, religion and other characteristics of a group of people

explorer: someone who travels in unknown regions

Governor General: the representative of the Queen in Canada, appointed on the advice of the Canadian Prime Minister

guest child: an English girl or boy who came to Canada during World War II to avoid the bombings in Britain

habitant: a French settler in early Quebec

heritage: a cultural background that is handed on to a person from his or her parents or ancestors

home child: a British girl or boy, often poor or orphaned, who came to Canada to work as farm or household help

homesteader: a settler who was given land on the prairies by the Canadian government in exchange for farming and building a home on it

immigrant: a person who comes to live in one country from another

Jewish war orphan: a Jewish child whose parents died in Europe during World War II. Some war orphans were cared for by Jewish Canadian families after the war.

les filles du roi: a French phrase meaning "daughters of the King," which referred to young women sent to Canada by the King of France to marry men (often soldiers) in New France

Loyalist: someone who stayed loyal to Britain during the American Revolution

Member of Parliament: a person elected to the federal parliament (government) in Ottawa; an MP

Métis: a person of Aboriginal and European ancestry

multicultural: a group made up of people from a mix of cultures and ethnic backgrounds

Order of Canada: an order of merit awarded to Canadians for outstanding achievements

post-war immigrant: a person who comes to live in one country after a war in his or her home country; often refers to an immigrant who came to Canada from Europe following World War II

refugee: a person who flees a country, due to war or persecution, in search of safety elsewhere

Senate: the upper branch of the federal government. A person appointed to the Senate is called a senator.

settler: someone who comes to settle or live in one country from another

slave: a person who is the property of someone else and has no rights of his or her own

war bride: a woman who married a Canadian soldier in Britain or Europe during World War I or II and came to Canada to live

war resister: a person, often called a "draft dodger," who protested against the Vietnam War and refused to serve in the United States army during that time. Thousands of war resisters fled to Canada.

INDEX

Aboriginal people, 6–7, 9, 19, 63
Acadians, 12–13
African immigrants, 31, 53
Ahenakew, Dr. Freda, 7
Alberta, 34
Alexander, Lincoln, 23
American Revolution, 14–15
anti-Semitism, 41
Asian immigrants, 26–31
Asian Ugandans, 53

Bangladesh, 30, 31
Barnardo, Thomas, 37
Bata, Thomas, 52
Battle of the Plains of Abraham, 13
Bernardi, Mario, 49
Birchtown (Nova Scotia), 15
Black Canadians, 15, 22–23, 25, 50–51
Black Loyalists, 15
Blucke, Colonel Stephen, 15
"boat people," 55
Bradshaw, Hilda, 43
British Columbia, 24–31, 57, 58
British immigrants and settlers, 8–9, 16–19, 36–37, 42, 43
Brooks, Kaarina, 39
Brown, Rosemary, 51

Cabot, John, 8
Canada
  as mosaic, 56
  top ten countries immigrants come from, 62
Canadian citizenship, 59
Canadian Pacific Railway, 26, 32
Caribana, 50
Caribbean immigrants, 31, 50–51
Cartier, Jacques, 8
Champlain, Samuel de, 8
children, 4–5, 20–21, 36–37, 42, 44, 60–61
Chilean refugees, 55
Chinese immigrants, 26–27, 57
Chinese Immigration Act, 26
Clapham, Robert, 37
Clarkson, Adrienne, 27
Clearances, 17, 18
"colonist" trains, 32, 39
concentration camps, 45, 47
"continuous passage" rule, 30–31
Czech refugees, 52

Dallaire, Roméo, 49
Datt, Shushma, 31
discrimination, 26, 28, 41, 50. See also racism
diseases, 20
displaced persons, 46–47, 63
Donnacona, 8
Dosanjh, Ujjal, 31
Douglas, James, 25
"draft dodgers," 52, 63
Dutch immigrants, 48, 49

English immigrants, 18–19, 36–37, 42–43
Ericsson, Leif, 7
European immigrants and refugees, 7–9, 32–35, 44–49, 52, 57
explorers, 8–9, 24

Fauconnier, Jeanne, 10–11
filles du roi, 10–11, 63
Fortune, Rose, 15
French settlers, 8–13
fur trade, 9, 25

Geikie, Archibald, 18
German immigrants, 14, 34–35, 40
gold rush, 24–25
Great Depression, 40
Great Potato Famine, 17
Gretzky, Wayne, 35
Grosse Île (Quebec), 21
guest children, 42

habitants, 10–11
Halifax, 38–39
Hawaiian settlers, 25
head tax, 26, 27
Hebert, Louis, 10–11
Henrìquez, Alicia, 58–59
Holocaust, 44–45
home children, 36–37
Hungarian refugees, 52

Icelandic immigrants, 32, 35
"ideal settlers," 40
illegal immigrants, 57
Immigrant Services Society, 58
immigrants, resentment towards, 28, 40–41
immigration laws
  made more inclusive, 26, 29, 31, 50, 54
  wartime restrictions, 40
immigration process, 38–39, 58–59
internment (prison) camps, 40
Irish immigrants, 16, 17, 19, 20–21
Italian immigrants, 41, 49

Jaffer, Mobina, 53
Jaffer, Rahim, 53
Japanese immigrants, 28–29, 41

Jean, Michaëlle, 51
Jewish immigrants, 44
Jewish refugees, 41, 44–45, 63
Jewish war orphans, 44–45
Jiménez, Antonio Saez, 39
Johl, Mrs. Pritam K., 31

"Kanakas," 25
  See also Hawaiian settlers
Keegan, Gerald, 21
Kerz, Anna, 47
King, William Lyon Mackenzie, 48
Kogawa, Joy, 29
Komagata Maru, 30–31
Kosovar refugees, 57
Kurelek, William, 35

language barrier, 58
Latin American refugees, 55, 58–59
Laumann, Silken, 35
Levalds, Ausma, 47
Levine, Karen, 45
Lewis, Daurene, 15
Lewis, Stephen, 45
Little, Mr. and Mrs. John, 23
Loyalists, 14–15, 34–35

Macdonald, Sir John A., 19
Maillet, Antonine, 13
Manak, Karm, 31
Manitoba, 32, 33, 48
Marchand, Leonard, 7
McClung, Nellie, 19
Mennonites, 33, 35
Métis, 7, 19, 63
Montreal, 12,
Moodie, Susanna and Dunbar, 19
Morissette, Alanis, 52
multiculturalism, 50, 54, 56

Nansen Medal, 55
New France, 8–13
New Iceland, 32
Newfoundland, 7, 8
Nova Scotia, 15, 38–39

Ontario, 34–37, 49
orphans, 20, 21, 36–37, 44–45
Overlanders, 25

Pakistan, 30, 31
Parlby, Irene, 19
Peterson, Oscar, 51
Phuc, Kim, 55
Pier 21, 38–39, 42
Polish immigrants, 34, 35
Porakyo, Sofie, 34
post-war immigrants, 48–49
Prairie provinces, 32–35

Quebec (city), 8, 10, 12, 13
Quebec (province), 12, 20–21.
  See also New France

racism, 51, 57
refugees, 41, 44–45, 52–53, 55, 57, 58–59
relocation camps, 28–29, 41
residential schools, 6
Riel, Louis, 7
riots, 28
Rollet, Marie, 10–11
Russian immigrants, 33

sailing ships, 20
Salvadorean refugees, 58–59
Sarabande, 47
Sauvé, Jeanne, 13
Schubert, Catherine and Augustus, 25
Scofield, Gregory, 19
Scottish immigrants, 17–19
Shadd, Mary Ann, 23
Sifton, Clifford, 33
slaves, 22–23
South Asian immigrants, 30–31
Sri Lanka, 30, 31
St. Louis, 41
Suzuki, David, 29

Taylor, Ted, 36
Toews, Miriam, 35
Torres-Cereceda, Hugo, 55
Toronto, 49
Tran, Hieu, 55
Trois-Rivières, 12
Trudeau, Pierre Elliott, 13, 54
Tryggvason, Bjarni, 35
Tubman, Harriet, 23

Ugandan refugees, 53
Ukrainian immigrants, 34, 35
Underground Railroad, 22–23
United States
  Black settlers from California, 25
  Loyalists, 14–15
  Mennonite settlers from, 35
  slaves escape from, 22–23
  war resisters from, 52

Vancouver, 28, 30–31, 54, 58
Verkaar, Maurice, 48
Vietnam War, 52
Vietnamese refugees, 55
Vikings, 7

Waisman, Robbie, 45
war brides, 43
war orphans, 44–45, 63
war resisters, 52, 63
Welcome House, 58
west coast, 24–25, 57, 58
Wilson, Hazel, 42
World War I, 40
World War II, 28, 41–47

Yee, Paul, 27

Znaimer, Moses, 45